HOUSE OF CARDS

HOUSE OF CARDS
Reforming America's Housing Finance System

EDITED BY SATYA THALLAM

MERCATUS CENTER
George Mason University

THE MERCATUS CENTER at George Mason University is the world's premier university source for market-oriented ideas—bridging the gap between academic ideas and real-world problems.

A university-based research center, Mercatus advances knowledge about how markets work to improve people's lives by training graduate students, conducting research, and applying economics to offer solutions to society's most pressing problems.

Our mission is to generate knowledge and understanding of the institutions that affect the freedom to prosper and to find sustainable solutions that overcome the barriers preventing individuals from living free, prosperous, and peaceful lives.

Founded in 1980, the Mercatus Center is located on George Mason University's Arlington campus.

www.mercatus.org

Copyright © 2012 by the Mercatus Center at George Mason University.
All rights reserved.

Mercatus Center, George Mason University
3351 Fairfax Drive, 4th Floor, Arlington, VA 22201-4433
T: (703) 993-4930

Printed in the United States of America
Reformatted second printing, July 2013

Library of Congress Cataloging-in-Publication Data

House of cards : reforming America's housing finance system / edited by Satya Thallam, Mercatus Center at George Mason University, Arlington, Virginia.
    pages cm
 Description based on second printing, 2013.
 Includes index.
 ISBN 978-0-9892193-2-7 (pbk.) -- ISBN 978-0-9836077-1-7 (e-book)
 1. Housing--United States--Finance. 2. Mortgage loans--United States.
I. Thallam, Satya.
 HD7293.Z9H66 2012
 332.7'220973--dc23
                        2013026865

CONTENTS

Foreword
Edward Glaeser   1

Editor's Note
Satya Thallam   5

Reforming the U.S. Mortgage Market
Through Private Market Incentives
Dwight M. Jaffee   17

Two Approaches to GSE Reform
Arnold Kling   61

A New Housing Finance System for the United States
Peter J. Wallison   91

The Way Forward: U.S. Residential-Mortgage
Finance in a Post-GSE World
Lawrence J. White   123

The Future of Fannie Mae and Freddie Mac
Michael Lea and Anthony B. Sanders   151

Do We Need the 30-Year Fixed-Rate Mortgage?
Michael Lea and Anthony B. Sanders   171

About the Contributors   195

Index   201

FOREWORD

EDWARD GLAESER

IN 2006, AT the height of the housing bubble, prescient voices—such as Dwight M. Jaffee's and Peter J. Wallison's—warned of the dangers inherent in allowing privately managed, profit-seeking government-sponsored enterprises (GSEs) to operate with implicit government guarantees. In those heady years, both the GSEs and homeowners racked up big paper profits, and they could ignore those correct Cassandras. In the wake of a great housing crash and the financial collapse of Fannie Mae and Freddie Mac, however, America's housing policies, particularly those related to the GSEs, must be rethought.

The past structure of the GSEs represented both a micro and a macro problem. The micro problem was specific to the incentives facing those entities. Whenever a private company that aims to make money operates with an implicit government guarantee, it will be able to borrow money at low rates unrelated to the risks that it takes. That structure practically guarantees excessive gambling.

The GSEs, borrowing at just a few basis points over Treasury rates, accumulated vast portfolios of retained mortgages and took on massive risks insuring trillions of dollars of mortgages. Their managers and shareholders stood to earn vast profits—as they did for many years—if their bets turned out well. If the bets turned sour, taxpayers would cover the losses. The hundreds of billions of dollars that ordinary Americans must pay now to cover the GSEs' losses is the unsurprising outcome of a misbegotten system.

But the GSEs are also symptomatic of a larger, macro problem in American housing policy: its fetish for subsidizing home-related borrowing. The implicit subsidy provided for the GSEs filtered down to home buyers and enabled them to borrow at artificially deflated rates. Accompanied by the borrowing subsidy created by the Home Mortgage Interest Deduction and rule changes that enabled home buyers to obtain a loan with just a minimal down payment, GSE policies subsidized leverage and encouraged Americans to borrow as much as possible to bet on the vicissitudes of the housing market. During the boom, all this home buying was lauded for creating an "ownership society." Now, it appears that these policies actually seem to have helped create a foreclosure society.

Homes do represent the primary form of wealth for many Americans, but that doesn't mean that subsidizing mortgage interest—either explicitly through the tax code or implicitly through the GSEs—encourages savings. Subsidizing borrowing actually encourages people to take money out of their houses by increasing the sizes of their loans. Lower down-payment requirements alleviate the need to save in order to buy a home.

Subsidizing home borrowing also distorts many other decisions. Not every American needs to be a homeowner. By subsidizing home borrowing, the government encourages Americans to invest too much in a single, volatile asset class. The government encourages Americans to buy and build larger homes, which makes little sense given that American homes are already extremely large by world standards and bigger homes typically mean more home energy use. Subsidizing home ownership also pushes people away from urban apartments, which are typically rentals, into suburban detached housing, which is typically owner-occupied.

While the problems of the existing system are obvious, the path forward is not. During the boom, the enemies of reform were able to marshal arguments—apparently compelling to many—about how the GSEs were necessary for housing markets to function. These arguments are still being put forward in defense of the GSEs.

Wall Street traders argue that GSE insurance is necessary to create a standardized, tradable product. Real estate industry advocates argue that without GSE subsidies, housing prices will drop still further and create more havoc for the American economy. And we should not forget that Congress's first response to the housing bust was to come up with a new housing subsidy—the Home Buyers' Tax Credit.

The prevalence of arguments in favor of the status quo only increases the need for good reform proposals. But any such reform proposal must face two great questions. First, will the proposal—as planned—manage to protect American taxpayers and sustain a functioning housing market? Second, will the proposal end up working as planned?

For example, some have called for simply privatizing Freddie Mac and Fannie Mae and getting them off the government's books. As planned, this strategy could enable the housing and securitization markets to function without government subsidies.

However, one can reasonably ask whether the government will be able to avoid providing an implicit guarantee for these reprivatized entities. They were, after all, privatized before, and yet they certainly had an implicit guarantee. Indeed, one can plausibly argue that taxpayers would have been safer if Freddie Mac and Fannie Mae had been entirely public institutions during the boom. In that case, they would have lacked the incentive to expand their business, taking on extra risks in order to make more profits.

As we approach the future, we need to move intelligently away from the mistakes of the past and toward a safer system that does less to distort housing markets and more to protect taxpayers. It is quite reasonable to argue that sensible reforms will have at worst a minor impact on prices. Given the abundance of secondary markets for debt, such as credit-card debt, that operate perfectly well without public insurance entities, it is quite reasonable to argue that private insurers can also produce standardized, securitized mortgages while not raising the risk posed by a large mortgage insurer of being too big to fail.

That is why the Mercatus Center's attempt to collect a series of good ideas for reform is enormously valuable. The proposals that follow provide a good basis for discussing the future of the GSEs and American housing finance.

EDITOR'S NOTE

SATYA THALLAM

THIS VOLUME IS a contribution to the ongoing debate on how to reform the country's housing-finance system in the wake of the 2008–2009 financial crisis. That crisis, from which the economy is still languishing, exposed fundamental flaws in the way we allocate scarce resources toward different uses, particularly housing. Taking one step back, however, the crisis should cause us to rethink the emphasis on homeownership that has pervaded national policy for several generations.

One prominent lever policy makers often pulled was Fannie Mae and Freddie Mac, often collectively referred to as the government-sponsored enterprises (GSEs). Within this volume, you will find six separate proposals on how to reform these mortgage-financing institutions and their mechanisms. Each proposal is distinct, though they share a common purpose. In each, the authors attempt to satisfy the same set of policy outcomes:

- To insulate taxpayers from additional future liabilities associated with the GSEs in their current form.

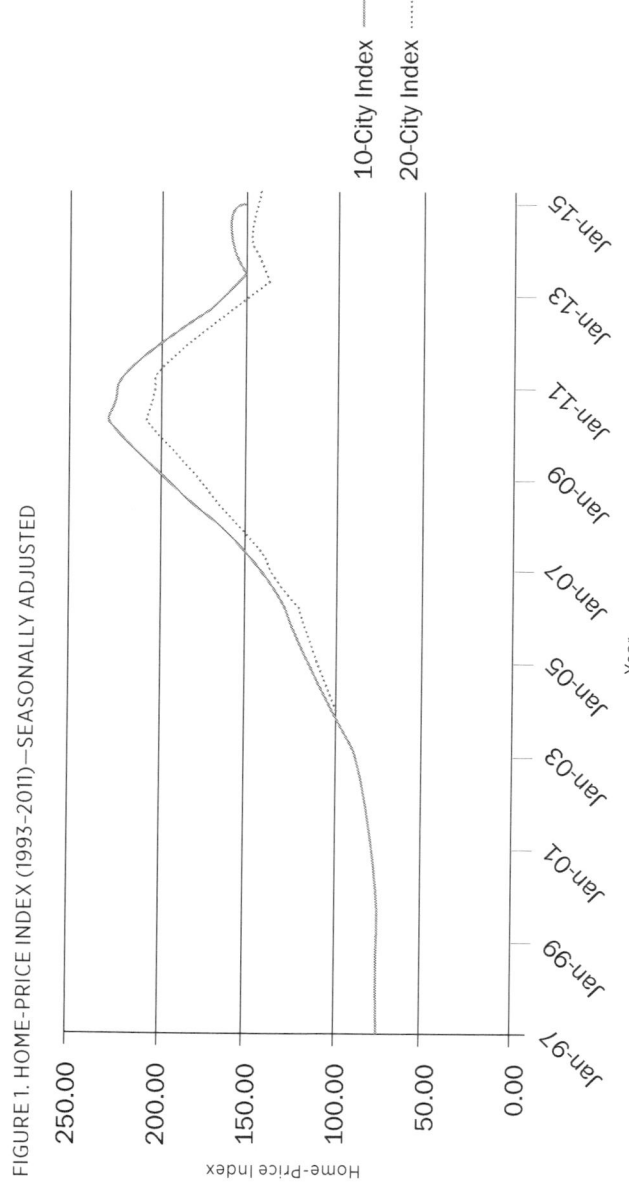

Source: S&P/Case-Shiller Home Price Index Levels, Seasonally Adjusted, February 2011

- To increase the role of private capital in financing mortgages.

- To maintain a safe and robust system to channel capital to able borrowers.

It should be noted that any proposal that substantially alters the contours of housing finance must be predicated, to some degree, on assumptions. A substantial federal government role began as far back as 1934, with the creation of the Federal Housing Administration (FHA). Since that time, the government's role in housing finance has consistently grown. This means no one reading this volume, or otherwise considering reform options, has likely ever experienced firsthand a primarily private marketplace for housing capital without significant government distortions. Fannie Mae and Freddie Mac have dominated the U.S. mortgage market for almost 40 years. Put another way, any reform that fundamentally alters the status quo of mortgage finance ultimately has to imagine a world in which we have never lived.

WHY THE FOCUS ON GSEs?

WHATEVER THE NUMEROUS and complex causes of the financial crisis and its attendant effects, mortgages were certainly at the heart of it all.[1] One estimate of the losses associated with loans and their securities held and issued by U.S. institutions is $3.6 trillion.[2] Fueled in part by a 12-year boom in nominal house prices (1993–2005),[3] demand for mortgage-backed instruments seemed to know no bound (see Figure 1).

One of the drivers of this trend was the weakening of lending standards at the GSEs. This led to purchasing riskier mortgages. For example, loans with a loan-to-value (LTV) ratio of greater than or equal to 97 percent are a broad measure of nontraditional and high-risk loans.

Loans with higher LTVs are riskier because they imply a higher rate of leverage.[4] A 97 percent LTV loan has a 3 percent down payment, whereas the GSEs had traditionally been in the business of buying and securitizing loans with 20 percent down payments and low credit-risk characteristics, also known as "prime loans." The share of Fannie Mae's home-purchase loans of high LTV skyrocketed around 2001, reaching nearly 40 percent in 2007 after being effectively 0 percent prior to 1996.[5]

Edward Pinto, former chief credit officer at Fannie Mae, explains the process by which this increase in leverage affects the entire housing market:

1. It leads to increased demand for housing by making more households eligible for loans, thereby moving down the demand curve.

2. This causes prices to rise.

3. Broadly rising prices inflate the equity of all homeowners, leading to more equity withdrawals.

4. This increase in equity withdrawals fuels economic growth, leading to more demand and further price increases.

5. Prices increase faster than income, creating an affordability gap that can be addressed only through weakening lending standards (more leverage).

6. More and more poor quality loans lead to an eventual—and painful—price correction.[6]

While the GSEs were loading their balance sheets with more and more of these risky loans, they were simultaneously leading the charge into the market, taking on a higher overall market share. Using a slightly different definition of risky loans—so-called nontraditional mortgages, the GSEs may have been responsible for a full 60 percent of this market—worth $4.6 trillion—as late as June 2008.[7] Michael Cembalest, chief investment officer at JPMorgan Chase, explains the effect this had on nonagency institutions:

> Housing policies instituted in the early 1990s were explicitly designed to require US Agencies *[sic]* to make much riskier loans, with the ultimate goal of pushing private sector banks to adopt the same standards. To be sure, private sector banks and investors are responsible for taking the bait, and made terrible mistakes. Overall, what emerges is an object lesson in well-meaning public policy gone spectacularly wrong.[8]

Cut to year-end 2009, and the GSEs' total debt and mortgage-backed securities obligations totaled $5.5 trillion, with a potential bailout cost of $400 billion.[9]

At the time of this writing, the House of Representatives Committee on Financial Services is considering a package of bills to stem the tide of losses from the GSEs and, subsequently, unwind their roles in mortgage finance.[10] While the proposals included in this volume are meant to be understood as attempts at comprehensive reform, they also implicitly acknowledge that reform may require piecemeal steps and, thus, include several separable ideas to that end. Whether comprehensive reform is preferable to marginal changes—much less whether it is politically possible—is outside the scope of this volume. Here, we present the intellectual arguments for reform and a variety of means to accomplish it in a productive way.

THE TRUE COST OF HOUSING

EVEN THE NUMBERS associated with a bailout of the GSEs are only their direct fiscal cost. Because of their funding advantages due to their unique hybrid status, we can assume that at least some of the capital driven toward funding mortgages would instead have provided a higher social return if invested somewhere else. This is not to say, of course, that all capital channeled through the GSEs was of this type—certainly some or perhaps much of the inframarginal investments in housing were optimal, that is, social-welfare maximizing. At the same time, the GSEs were only a part of the larger policy apparatus that incentivized investment in housing, including the tax code and local land-use regulations among others.

Much of the resistance to housing-finance reform is constrained by worries that housing investment and homeownership will decrease.[11] Thus, it is worth considering the larger picture of whether, from a societal point of view, we would indeed be better off if we invested less in housing.

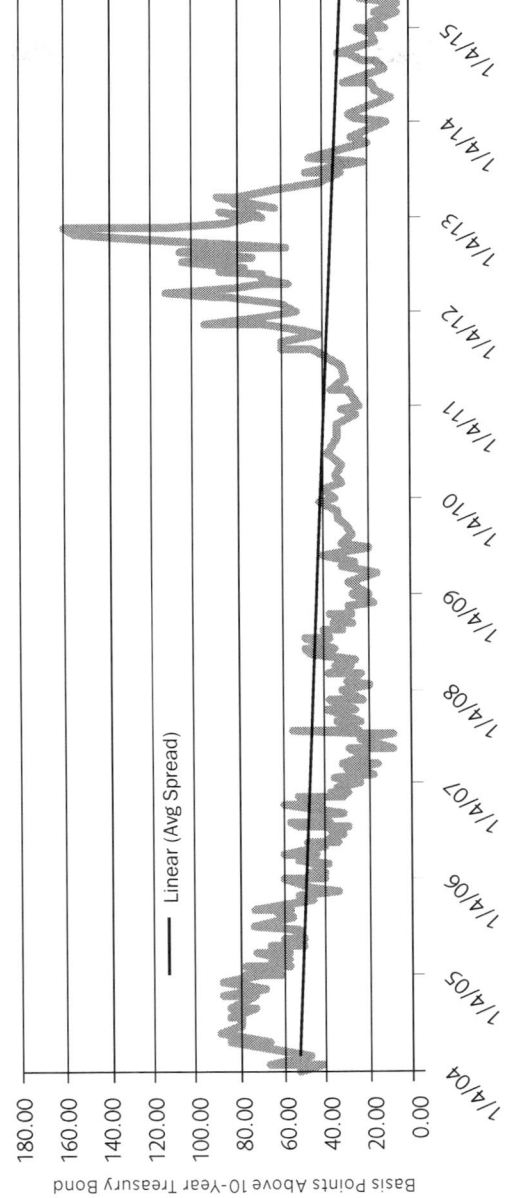

FIGURE 2. AVERAGE OF FANNIE MAE AND FREDDIE MAC DEBT SPREADS OVER 10-YEAR TREASURY

Source: Anthony B. Sanders, "Fannie/Freddie Is Shadow Treasury Debt – and Behaving Like It!" *Confounded Interest*, April 8, 2011, http://confoundedinterest.wordpress.com/2011/04/08/fanniefreddie-is-shadow-treasury-debt-and-behaving-like-it.

With respect to private rates of return, we expect incentives to channel private investments to where its return is highest.[12] But the social rate of return may be different due to the effect of social policies. As former Dallas Fed senior economist Lori Taylor puts it, "While market arbitrage ensures that risk-adjusted private rates of return equalize, no similar mechanism exists to guarantee that social rates of return do the same. Thus, society may invest relatively too much in some types of capital and relatively too little in others."[13] If the social rate of return to housing is less than other uses, this means we are forgoing more productive investments and, ultimately, allocating capital in a suboptimal manner and experiencing less economic growth.

The prominent urban economist Edwin S. Mills uses the national income accounts data to calculate a first-order approximation of the aggregate return to housing capital. His model assumes a two-sector economy with two types of capital investments: housing and nonhousing. In an optimal allocation, the return on investment to one will equal the return on the other.[14]

The rate of return to housing capital will be the sum of aggregate rents as a share of total housing capital plus capital gains. The rate of return to nonhousing capital will be the remainder of national output (less housing) as a share of capital plus capital gains.

Over the period 1929–86, Mills finds the social rate of return to housing was one-fifth that of nonhousing capital.[15] Taylor extends the analysis to the period 1975–95 and makes adjustments for risk. She finds the relative returns are similar to Mills: "The unmeasured benefit to housing investment would have to top $220 billion per year (or

$300 per month for each owner-occupied home) to support the current allocation of resources."[16]

THE DISAPPEARING YIELDS PROBLEM

HAVING BEEN IN attendance at many of the recent congressional committee hearings related to reform of the nation's housing-finance system, I repeatedly heard members of Congress inquire as to how we can implement reforms which "crowd in" private capital. With the GSEs and FHA representing a combined market share of over 90 percent of the existing mortgage market, they wonder whether private capital will or can return to pick up the slack should the federal government's involvement be reduced over time.

But the follow-on worry is that the cost of funds for mortgages will rise. Well, yes, but that's sort of the point. As Figure 2 shows, the yields on GSE debt are very low—in the range of 20-basis points above Treasuries's range. They are so low that, to investors, they are effectively the same as Treasuries. This might make them attractive to some low-risk bond investors, but they are unacceptably low to the private capital holders that policy makers worry about "getting into the game." In the absence of the GSEs (in their current form), we expect yields on mortgage funds to rise, which will make them relatively more attractive to private-capital investors. Moreover, the cost of funds will rise to reflect risk more accurately, compared to the artificially low levels at which GSEs pushed these funds over the years leading up to the crisis. But none of this can happen unless the GSEs discontinue crowding out private capital.[17]

CONCLUSION

A MORE THOROUGH investigation of the role of Fannie Mae and Freddie Mac in the housing-finance system—pre-and post crisis—is outside the scope of this volume but can be found elsewhere.[18] What this volume offers is a way forward from what most people agree is an unsustainable status quo. What follows are six separate proposals on how to reform the housing-finance system in ways that are productive yet sensitive to the United States's fragile recovery. Housing will continue to be, as it has been for many decades, a large and crucial part of the American economy. But the methods that channel available capital to borrowers absolutely must be reformed such that we are not susceptible to another artificial bubble and subsequent crash. In the aftermath of the 2008–2009 financial crisis, we may be experiencing an opportune moment to further these ends.

NOTES

1. There were no doubt several sources of trouble, see Financial Crisis Inquiry Commission, "Causes of the Financial and Economic Crisis: Dissenting Statement of Keith Hennessey, Douglas Holtz-Eakin, and Bill Thomas," http://fcic-static.law.stanford.edu/cdn_media/fcic-reports/fcic_final_report_hennessey_holtz-eakin_thomas_dissent.pdf. See also Arnold Kling, *Not What They Had in Mind: A History of Policies that Produced the Financial Crisis of 2008* (Arlington, VA: Mercatus Center at George Mason University, 2009).
2. Nouriel Roubini and Elisa Parisi-Capone, "Total $3.6 Trillion Projected Loan and Securities Losses in the U.S., $1.8 Trillion of Which Borne by U.S. Banks/Brokers: Specter of Technical Insolvency for the Banking System Calls for Comprehensive Solution," RGE Monitor, January 2009, http://media.rgemonitor.com/papers/0/RGECreditLossesEPCNRJan09.pdf.
3. S&P/Case-Shiller Home Price Indices, "Home-Price Index Levels: February 2011," http://www.standardandpoors.com/indices/sp-case-shiller-home-price-indices/en/us/?indexId=spusa-cashpidff--p-us----.

4. The LTV ratio of a loan is not the only indication of its relative riskiness; it is just one characteristic. Others are the credit history and FICO score of the borrower as well as the borrower's debt and income status.

5. Edward J. Pinto, "Government Housing Policies in the Lead-up to the Financial Crisis: A Forensic Study," American Enterprise Institute, August 14, 2010, 26, chart 15.

6. Ibid., 22–24.

7. Ibid.

8. Michael Cembalest, "Eye on the Market," JPMorgan, May 3, 2011, 3.

9. Government Accountability Office (GAO), "Fannie Mae and Freddie Mac: Analysis of Options for Revising the Housing Enterprises' Long-Term Structures," GAO Report 09-782, September 10, 2009, http://www.gao.gov/products/GAO-09-782.

10. The first round of these bills was considered in subcommittee April 5, 2011. Indications are, however, there are many political obstacles to these proposals, see Alan Fram, "Ill Housing Markets Trump Ideology for Many in GOP," *Associated Press*, April 25, 2011.

11. For example see Committee on Financial Services, "Congresswoman Waters Concerned about Future of Homeownership in GSE Reform Proposals," press release, February 11, 2011, http://democrats.financialservices.house.gov/press/PRArticle.aspx?NewsID=1398.

12. We also expect arbitrage transactions in liquid markets to equalize the relative returns between investments.

13. Lori L. Taylor, "Does the United States Still Overinvest in Housing?" *Economic Review*, Federal Reserve Bank of Dallas, second quarter, 1998.

14. Edwin S. Mills, "Social Returns to Housing and Other Fixed Capital," *Real Estate Economics*, 17, issue 2 (June 1989): 197–211.

15. Ibid.

16. Taylor, "Does the United States Still Overinvest in Housing?"

17. Admittedly, the question of how public capital and private capital interact (as substitutes, complements, or some variation of the two) is not fully settled. In some research, public capital is more accurately thought of as different types which each have a different effect. See, for instance, Luis Serven, "Does Public Capital Crowd Out Private Capital? Evidence from India, Volume 1," *Policy Research Working Paper no. WPS 1613*, World Bank: Human Development and Public Services, May 31, 1996.

18. For a very thorough treatment of this issue, see Pinto, "Government Housing Policies in the Lead-up to the Financial Crisis: A Forensic Study."

REFORMING THE U.S. MORTGAGE MARKET THROUGH PRIVATE MARKET INCENTIVES

DWIGHT M. JAFFEE*

FOR ALMOST 40 years, Fannie Mae and Freddie Mac dominated the U.S. mortgage market based on their status as government-sponsored enterprises (GSEs). By 2008, however, the U.S. mortgage and housing markets had crashed, and the two GSEs survived only as the result of a government bailout and conservatorship.[1] At year-end 2009, the GSEs' total debt and mortgage-backed securities (MBS) obligations had reached $5.5 trillion, and the cost to taxpayers of the GSE bailout could reach $400 billion.[2]

Although the subprime crash devastated the GSEs, their dominance of the U.S. mortgage market actually expanded: During 2009 and 2010 as much as 70 percent of mortgage-market activity was carried out through the GSEs, and another 25 percent was guaranteed through the Federal Housing Administration (FHA) and U.S.

---

* I thank the three anonymous reviewers of this chapter for their useful and constructive comments.

Department of Veterans Affairs (VA).[3] This expanded government role reflects the intense use of the GSEs and of the FHA and Government National Mortgage Association (GNMA) as policy instruments to revive the mortgage market.[4] Some commentators suggest that a private market for U.S. mortgages is no longer possible. More accurately, however, most private mortgage-market activity has simply been crowded out by the now heavily subsidized government programs.

The goal of this paper is to look beyond the current crisis and analyze proposals for long-term reform of the U.S. mortgage market. Following the structure of this volume, it is assumed the GSEs are abolished and play no further role within the U.S. mortgage market.[5] This chapter lays out a specific proposal to reform the U.S. mortgage market by applying purely private-market incentives for mortgage originators, securitizers, and investors while retaining the FHA and U.S. Department of Housing and Urban Development (HUD) programs in support of lower-income, first-time, and other special classes of home buyers.[6] The analysis develops the case that private incentives and institutions are sufficient to create a functional and efficient mortgage market, while eliminating the need for taxpayer subsidies and bailouts. The discussion marshals the evidence that stable housing and mortgage activity can be sustained with minimal governmental intervention, including data demonstrating the success in western European housing and mortgage markets. The discussion concludes with an evaluation of alternative proposals to reform the U.S. mortgage market.

REFORMING THE U.S. MORTGAGE MARKET WITHOUT GSES

REFORMING THE U.S. mortgage market continues to be a critical policy issue. While the Dodd-Frank 2010 Financial Reform Act took no significant action in this regard, the U.S. Department of the Treasury and HUD recently released a new white paper that provides a framework for mortgage-market reform.[7] The proposal evaluated in this section fits within the Treasury/HUD white paper framework as the "private-market" solution to reorganizing the U.S. mortgage market, with private-market incentives and institutions taking the place of the GSEs. Success will be achieved if the private markets create stable and accessible mortgage credit for U.S. borrowers without requiring taxpayer subsidies or bailouts.

A Proposal to Reform the U.S. Mortgage Market along Private-Market Principles[8]

THE PROPOSAL ADVOCATED here would be implemented with just two actions:

1. Reduce the conforming loan limit—the maximum loan the GSEs may acquire or guarantee—each year until the limit reaches zero and GSE activity disappears. If the conforming loan limit is reduced by $100,000 per year, it will reach zero in approximately seven years. This also approximates the average duration of a U.S. mortgage, so most of the mortgage portfolios currently on GSE balance sheets would be off by that time as well. Steadily

reducing the conforming limit has three further advantages:

- It provides an orderly and smooth transition. In particular, private-market lenders and investors will know the GSE domain is shrinking and should be ready to substitute for it.

- The substitution of private-market activity for the GSEs would be observable. If it were failing to occur, alternative actions could be taken.

- The GSE subsidy is removed first from the largest mortgages, thereby maintaining the GSE benefit longest for lower-income borrowers.

2. The existing FHA and HUD programs supporting lower-income households continue under this proposal. These programs will provide a safety net should the private-market system fail to satisfy borrower needs as the GSEs retrench. These programs would also be available should a future financial crisis require new, temporary government support of the mortgage market.

GSE activity could also be reduced by requiring the GSEs to steadily raise their guarantee fees until they are priced out of the market.[9] This device could substitute for, or expand upon, the proposal to reduce the conforming loan limits. The discussion here focuses on the proposal to reduce the conforming loan size because it is simple and readily verifiable.

The Functional Structure of the U.S. Mortgage Market

TO CREATE ACCESSIBLE credit, a mortgage market must coordinate three basic functions:

1. originating new mortgages,
2. designing mortgage contracts and setting underwriting standards, and
3. placing the originated mortgages with long-term investors.

This section addresses how these activities are currently carried out and provides introductory comments on how they might change under a private mortgage market.

Origination of New Mortgages

THE ORIGINATION OF new mortgages in the United States has always been carried out entirely by private firms, even in the presence of the GSEs and the government's FHA and VA programs. In fact, the GSEs' charters prohibit them from originating mortgages, and the FHA and VA programs only insure mortgages that are originated to their specifications by private-market firms. Terminating the GSEs will, thus, have no direct impact on which firms will originate U.S. mortgages.

Mortgage Design and Underwriting Standards

THE GSEs HAVE always set the contract design and underwriting standards for the loans they acquired.[10] In

FIGURE 1. SHARE OF TOTAL WHOLE MORTGAGES AND MBS, BY HOLDER CLASS

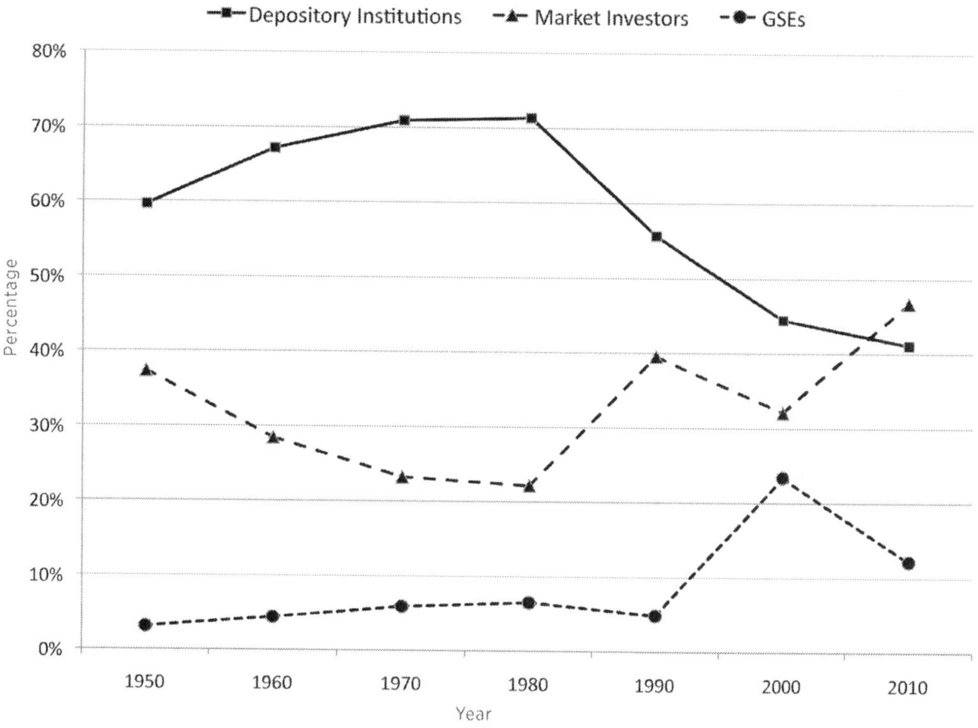
Depository Institutions
Market Investors
GSEs
80%
70%
60%
50%
40%
30%
20%
10%
0%
Percentage
1950
1960
1970
1980
1990
2000
2010
Year

Sources: Federal Reserve, Flow of Funds Accounts of the United States *(2010), http://www.federalreserve.gov/RELEASES/z1/Current/data.htm; Federal Housing Finance Agency,* Report to Congress *(2009); Fannie Mae,* Annual Report *(2010); and Freddie Mac Annual Report (2010).*

the reformed system, the contract design and standards will be set by the private market alone. Since mortgages will be originated only if there are willing final investors, these investors will ultimately set the designs and standards. Given that a significant share of all U.S. mortgage originations has always been placed *outside* the GSEs, the change is more of a degree than of a kind. Specifically, as the private market replaces the GSEs, mortgage choice will expand and overall underwriting standards for U.S. mortgages are likely to rise significantly, that is, mortgages will generally be safer.

The Mortgage Investment Function

THE THIRD FUNDAMENTAL mortgage-market function is to place the originated mortgages with long-term investors. Figure 1 shows the percentage of all U.S. home mortgages and related securities held by the three primary investor categories—depository institutions, market investors, and the GSEs—at the end of each decade as available over the last 60 years. The year 2010 represents the most recently available year-end data. Figure 1 is unique in that it integrates the holdings of whole mortgages and MBS and then computes the respective market shares as a percentage of total home-mortgages outstanding.

Between 1950 and 1980, the depository institutions—commercial banks, thrift institutions, and credit unions—held the vast majority of home mortgages, almost entirely as whole mortgages. The depository institutions were also the primary originators of home mortgages.[11] The depository institutions thus combined the activities of origination and investing. This "make them and hold them" model completely dominated the U.S. mortgage market through 1970.

Several major events occurred in the U.S. mortgage markets around 1970:

1. In 1968, GNMA was created within HUD to issue the first modern MBS. GNMA only securitizes FHA and VA mortgages.

2. Also in 1968, Fannie Mae was transformed from a government office within HUD to a public-private hybrid; it became a GSE.

3. In 1970, Freddie Mac was created as a second GSE.[12]

These three events initiated the mortgage securitization that has dominated the U.S. mortgage markets ever since. Following the prototype created by GNMA, Freddie Mac quickly added its own brand of MBS, called PC, and by the early 1980s Fannie Mae was also issuing its own MBS. Only the GNMA MBS had an official government guarantee against losses from borrower default, but the GSEs' MBS traded as if there were a strong, albeit implicit, government guarantee. Indeed, the three sets of MBS became collectively known as "agency" MBS. As the last step, by the mid-1980s, private-market firms were creating their own MBS brands, known as Private Label Securities (PLS). Because these securities had no government guarantee of any form, they applied the innovation of structured finance, whereby the default risk was allocated differentially across the various tranches, with the senior tranche protected by the subordinated junior tranche. The most knowledgeable and risk-tolerant investors purchased the junior tranche—thus taking on the first-loss position—and were compensated with an appropriately higher interest rate.

The key fact of Figure 1 is the dominance by 2010 of market investors and commercial banks as holders of nearly all U.S. whole mortgages and MBS—a combined 88 percent market share—while the retained mortgage portfolios of Fannie Mae and Freddie Mac represent only 12 percent of the total. The mortgage investments of the "market investors" in Figure 1 are computed as the residual category. Their growth begins in 1980 and is almost entirely represented by MBS positions, both agency MBS and PLS MBS.

This investor category includes mutual funds, real estate investment trusts, property and life insurers, pension and retirement funds, and foreign investors. The list demonstrates how mortgage-backed securitization achieved the benefit of expanding the class of investors far beyond the depositories who, otherwise, had to hold all the whole-home mortgages they originated directly. By 2010, these market investors were holding 47 percent of all U.S. home mortgages.

The implication is that gradually running off the GSE mortgage portfolios—over the approximately seven-year period proposed here—should be accomplished without any major stress in the flow of funds for U.S. mortgages. It should not be a serious problem for either the market investors or the commercial banks to replace the 12 percentage point market share left by terminating the GSEs.[13] For example, in the European mortgage market, commercial banks hold the majority of home mortgages, funded either with deposits or, to a significant degree, by covered bonds issued to capital-market investors. Covered bonds provide an alternative instrument to securitization for funding bank-originated mortgages with financial-market resources.

In this context, it is important to recognize that private-label securitization was highly successful from its origins in the mid-1980s until the subprime mortgage crash. Through 2006, if PLS MBS credit ratings changed at all, the changes were generally upgrades, not downgrades. The same is true for the loan securitizations that expanded into auto loans, credit card loans, and commercial MBS. The losses suffered on subprime MBS actually represent the first time large losses had hit any major class of U.S. securitizations. The subprime crash does not signify a problem with securitization per se, but with the poor quality of the underlying subprime mortgages; indeed, large losses occurred on subprime mortgages whether the loans were securitized or not. As a result, securitization continues to be an effective instrument for transferring mortgages from originators to third-party investors, and securitized mortgage-pool performance is likely to return to its historically positive record as soon as the quality of the underlying mortgages does the same.

In summary, all mortgage investments start in the capital markets—whether through bank depositors, covered bonds, the GSE-retained portfolios, or direct MBS investments—and a restriction in one channel is generally and easily offset by growth in the other channels. For this reason, elimination of the GSEs' on-balance-sheet portfolios is a minor concern.

The Performance of the U.S. Mortgage Market without GSEs

WHILE ABOLISHING THE GSEs creates no significant flow-of-funds issues, the quality of the mortgage and MBS assets that will be available in the market remains in question. At year-end 2010, home mortgage MBS outstanding totaled $6.6 trillion, of which $4.3 trillion or 65 percent, had been issued by the two GSEs. Most investors in these GSE MBS relied on the associated implicit Treasury guarantee, so they ignored the default risk embedded in the underlying mortgages. Following the GSE Conservatorships in September 2008, the implicit guarantees became effective, essentially making these investors home free. Under the proposal here, however, these assets will mature and new MBS will be issued by private firms without any form of government guarantee. What will happen then? The answer comes in two parts.

The first part assumes that the quality of U.S. mortgages remains unchanged. In this case, investors must directly face the default risk embedded in these mortgages and, therefore, will purchase them only with a higher yield. As a result, U.S. mortgage interest rates will rise. Most empirical studies indicate that the mortgage interest rates on GSE-conforming mortgages were approximately 25 basis points (bps) below the interest rates on equivalent mortgages that could not be acquired or guaranteed by the GSEs. Some studies suggest an even lower differential between GSE and private mortgages.[14] Even using the 25 bps spread, however, the amount seems quite minor given that mortgage interest rates commonly fluctuate by full percentage points as the result of macroeconomic shifts in the financial markets. Furthermore,

TABLE 1. THE PERFORMANCE OF EUROPEAN MORTGAGE MARKETS IN COMPARISON WITH THE U.S., 1998 TO 2010[1]

Country	Rate of Owner occupancy Latest Year (%)	Coefficient of Covariation Housing Starts (%) [2]	Standard Deviation of House-price Inflation (%)
Western Europe			
Austria	57.5	7.2	2.7
Belgium	78.0	15.2	7.4
Denmark	53.6	56.1	8.5
Finland	59.0	11.9	3.8
France	57.8	17.4	6.2
Germany	43.2	29.0	1.7
Ireland	74.5	99.2	14.2
Italy	80.0	25.7	3.4
Luxembourg	70.4	17.9	4.7
Netherlands	55.5	14.5	6.5
Norway	85.0	24.6	5.0
Portugal	74.6	35.5	2.9
Spain	85.0	93.0	8.1
Sweden	66.0	45.5	2.9
United Kingdom	66.4	25.0	6.8
European Average	**67.1**	**34.5**	**5.6**
United States	**66.9**	**45.5**	**7.3**
U.S. rank	**8th of 16**	**3rd of 16**	**5th of 16**

NOTES:

(1) Unless noted otherwise, the data are all from European Mortgage Federation (2009), an annual fact book that contains comprehensive mortgage and housing market data for the years 1998 to 2009 for 15 Western European countries and the United States.

(2) Computation based on housing starts where available; all other countries use housing permits.

(3) The mortgage interest rate spread equals the mortgage interest rate (column 4) relative to the each country's 3-month Treasury Bill rate; Source OECD Economic Outlook Database.

Mortgage Interest Rate Average Level (%)	Mortgage Interest Rate Average Spread (%) [3]	Outstanding Mortgage-to-GDP Ratio 2010 (%)
4.83	1.79	28.0
5.61	2.58	46.3
5.80	2.58	101.4
4.13	1.09	42.3
4.83	1.80	41.2
5.07	2.05	46.5
4.32	1.15	87.1
4.70	1.56	22.7
4.08	1.05	44.7
5.08	2.06	107.1
6.11	1.44	70.3
4.43	1.35	66.3
4.16	1.08	64.0
3.75	0.91	81.8
5.12	0.93	85.0
4.80	**1.56**	**62.3**
5.07	**2.26**	**76.5**
6th of 16	**3rd of 16**	**6th of 16**

the GSE subsidy came at a huge cost to U.S. taxpayers: current estimates suggest that the final GSE losses may cost U.S. taxpayers upwards of $400 billion. Thus, a 25 bps cost seems a low price to pay to avoid the taxpayer subsidies and costs of maintaining the GSEs.

The second part of the answer is even more optimistic. It reflects the fact that private-market lenders and investors will pay much more attention to the quality of new mortgage loans than they did under the GSE-dominated market. The GSEs discouraged risk-based pricing in the mortgage market: they either accepted or rejected the mortgage loans they evaluated. It was basically a pass-fail system. As most professors can attest, this leads to lower overall performance compared to a system in which superior performance is properly rewarded. A private-market system will charge lower mortgage rates on safer mortgages and higher mortgage rates on riskier mortgages. The outcome will be a market with overall safer mortgages, which implies lower overall mortgage interest rates.

Of course, the question of whether the shift to safer mortgages will actually dominate the loss of the 25 bps subsidy provided by the GSEs to conforming mortgage borrowers is an empirical one. Fortunately, there is a large and long-standing marketplace that can provide useful insights into the likely answer: most of the countries of western Europe have mortgage markets that have operated for many years with minimal government intervention—and certainly without government intervention at the level of the U.S. GSEs. The mortgage interest rates in these countries are generally lower than those created by the GSE-dominated system in the United States. In fact, the performance of the western European mortgage and housing markets is superior to that of the United States on basically all relevant measures.

WESTERN EUROPEAN MORTGAGE AND HOUSING MARKETS[15]

IT HAS BEEN more than 30 years since the U.S. mortgage markets operated without a significant presence of GSEs, so an immediate question is whether a private market can adequately provide the mortgage origination and investment services required by a large and dynamic housing market. Fortunately, the mortgage markets of western Europe have operated for decades with limited government intervention and, thus, provide a ready-made laboratory to observe the efficiency and effectiveness of essentially private housing and mortgage markets.[16]

The Performance of Western European Housing and Mortgage Markets[17]

TABLE 1 COMPARES the U.S. and western European mortgage markets for a range of quantitative attributes from 1998 to 2010 based on a comprehensive database of housing and mortgage data for 15 European countries from the European Mortgage Federation.[18]

Column 1 compares the 2009 owner-occupancy rates for the United States and European countries. The U.S. value is 67.2 percent, which is just below its peak subprime boom value. It is frequently suggested that the high rate of homeownership results from the large U.S. government support of the mortgage market, including the GSEs. It is

TABLE 2. TROUBLED MORTGAGES IN WESTERN EUROPE AND THE UNITED STATES

Country	≥ 3-Month Arrears (%)	Impaired or Doubtful (%)	Foreclosures (%)	Year
Belgium	0.46			2009
Denmark	0.53			2009
France		0.93		2008
Ireland	3.32			2009
Italy		3.00		2008
Portugal	1.17			2009
Spain		3.04	0.24	2009
Sweden		1.00		2009
United Kingdom	2.44		0.19	2009
U.S. All Loans	9.47		4.58	2009
U.S. Prime	6.73		3.31	2009
U.S. Subprime	25.26		15.58	2009

Source: European Mortgage Federation, "Methodological Note and Survey on Non-performing Loans in the EU," EMF Study, March 2010; Mortgage Bankers of America, "National Delinquency Survey," http://www.mortgagebankers.org/ResearchandForecasts/ProductsandSurveys/NationalDelinquencySurvey.htm.

revealing that the U.S. rate is just at the median—eighth out of the 16 developed countries—and equals the average value for the European countries precisely. Further, the lower owner-occupancy rates in some of the countries, Germany for example, appear to be the result of cultural preferences rather than government inaction. A full analysis of the determinants of owner-occupancy rates across countries should also control for the age distribution of the population, since younger households and possibly the oldest households may have lower ownership rates in all countries. Chirui and Jappelli provide a start in this direction, showing that lower down-payment rates are a significant factor encouraging owner occupancy after controlling for the population age structure in a sample of 14 Organisation for Economic Co-operation and Development (OECD) countries.[19] The United States has also generally benefitted from very low down-payment rates, but it still has an average ownership rate, reinforcing the conclusion that government interventions largely have been ineffective in raising the U.S. homeownership rate relative to its peers.

Column 2 measures the volatility of housing construction activity from 1998 to 2009 based on the coefficient of variation of housing starts as a measure of relative volatility. U.S. relative volatility is the fifth highest of the 16 countries, implying that government interventions have failed to reduce U.S. housing cycles relative to those in western Europe.

Column 3 measures the volatility of changes in house prices based on the standard deviation of the annual house-price appreciation from 1998 through 2009. Here the United States stands fourth, meaning the country has a relatively high rate of house-price volatility. This negative result is all the more significant because the United States is much larger than any of the individual western European countries and, thus, regional diversification should have lowered observed U.S. house-price volatility.

Column 4 compares the level of mortgage interest rates in western Europe and the United States using "representative variable mortgage rates" for western Europe and the Freddie Mac one-year adjustable-rate mortgage (ARM) commitment rate for the United States.[20] The column shows that the United States had the sixth highest average mortgage interest rate from 1998 to 2010. Since overall interest rates also vary across countries, column 5 shows the average spread between the mortgage rate and the Treasury-bill rate for each country. The United States ranks third highest based on the spread and exceeds the western European average by 70 bps. Of course, mortgage-contract terms, such as down-payment requirements, also vary by country, and the resulting variations in mortgage risk will be reflected in mortgage rates.[21] Below, the paper returns to the question of underwriting standards in a reformed U.S. mortgage market. For now, the primary conclusion is that U.S. government mortgage-market interventions have failed to improve access to homeownership through the channel of lower mortgage rates.[22]

Finally, column 6 shows the 2010 ratio of home mortgages outstanding to each country's annual GDP, a standard measure of the depth of a country's mortgage market. The U.S. ratio is 76.5 percent, putting it sixth within this group of 16 developed economies. A relatively high U.S. result is not surprising given the large mortgage subsidies provided through the GSEs and other channels. It is noteworthy that five western European countries achieved even higher ratios without substantial government interventions in their mortgage markets.[23]

Mortgage defaults are a remaining—and important—mortgage-market attribute to consider when comparing western European and U.S. mortgage markets. Table 2 tabulates the available recent data on mortgages in arrears, impaired, or in foreclosure for available western European countries and the United States. The most dramatic difference between western Europe and the United States is in the foreclosure rate. The U.S. foreclosure rate at year-end 2009 was 4.58 percent for all

TABLE 3. GOVERNMENT MORTGAGE PROGRAMS

Country	Government Mortgage Insurer	Government Security Guarantees	Government-Sponsored Enterprises
Denmark	No	No	No
Germany	No	No	No
Ireland	No	No	No
Netherlands	NHG	No	No
Spain	No	No	No
United Kingdom	No	No	No
Australia	No	No	No
Canada	CMHC	CMHC	No
Japan	No	JHF	Possible
Korea	No	No	Korean Housing Finance Corp.
Switzerland	No	No	No
United States	FHA	GNMA	Fannie Mae, Freddie Mac, FHLBs

Source: Michael Lea, "International Comparison of Mortgage Product Offerings," Research Institute for Housing America and Mortgage Bankers Association, September 2010, http://www.housingamerica.org/RIHA/RIHA/Publications/74023_10122_Research_RIHA_Lea_Report.pdf.

mortgages and 3.31 percent for prime mortgages—not to mention 15.58 percent for subprime mortgages. In contrast, Spain and the United Kingdom are two of the most distressed countries, but their foreclosure rates are 0.24 percent and 0.19 percent, respectively. Ireland is the other western European country currently facing serious mortgage distress as shown by its high rate of mortgage arrears in Table 2. Ginsberg and Turner report, however, that actual foreclosure rates in Ireland remain very low.[24] More generally, the European Central Bank states, "borrowers in euro area countries do not generally have major incentives to default on a mortgage, since they remain personally liable for any difference between the value of the property and the amount of the loan."[25]

The clear conclusion is that European mortgage default activity is benign compared with the United States. To be clear, countries such as Iceland, Ireland, Greece, Portugal, and Spain are facing major banking crises. However, domestic mortgage defaults are not a primary source of their bank difficulties: if the bank losses are at all related to real estate, they primarily arise from construction loans or commercial mortgages, not residential mortgages.

Western European residential mortgage and housing markets have outperformed the U.S. markets over the full range of available measures. Although data are not provided here, a similar conclusion would hold for the Australian, Canadian, and New Zealand mortgage markets. The next section considers the factors that created the superior performance in European and other countries.

The Unique Features of Western European Mortgage Markets[26]

WHAT FEATURES OF western European mortgages or mortgage markets have created this outstanding performance? This section considers a range of possible answers: government intervention, MBS versus covered bond systems, and mortgage-contract terms and conditions.

Government Intervention[27]

GIVEN THE MULTIDIMENSIONAL structure of government interventions in mortgage markets, no single metric can provide a complete comparison of the western European countries with the United States. It is possible, however, to distinguish at least three separate channels for government intervention and make comparisons one channel at a time. The channels are:

1. Government support for low-income mortgage borrowers,

2. Direct purchases/guarantees of middle-market mortgages by GSEs, and

3. Indirect government support for the mortgage market.

We shall see that the level of U.S. government support generally exceeds the European average and the extent of the U.S. government interventions often exceeds that of all of the European countries (see Table 3). The superior European performance has been achieved with very modest government support.

- **Support for low-income borrowers.** The U.S. mortgage reform proposal this paper recommends would continue the existing FHA and HUD programs that provide mortgage and housing-market support for lower-income families. Furthermore, it appears that the United States and western European countries carry out a similar range of

TABLE 4. 2009 RATIO OF COVERED BONDS TO RESIDENTIAL MORTGAGES OUTSTANDING

Country	Percentage
Austria	7.3
Belgium	N.A.
Denmark	100.0
Finland	6.5
France	23.9
Germany	19.6
Ireland	20.1
Italy	4.2
Luxembourg	0.0
Netherlands	4.7
Norway	26.3
Portugal	18.5
Spain	49.6
Sweden	56.7
United Kingdom	14.7

Source: European Covered Bonds Council, ECBC Factbook, 5th ed. 2010, http://ecbc.hypo.org/Content/default.asp?PageID=501.

programs in support of lower-income households. The conclusion is that government programs in support of lower-income borrowers are not a differentiating factor with regard to the performance of the European mortgage markets.

- **GSE activity.** No European government entity's role approaches the dominance of the GSEs in the U.S. mortgage market. In the absence of GSEs, almost all western European mortgage lending is carried out privately by banks and funded by bank deposits and covered bonds.[28]

- **Indirect government support.** Governments may support their mortgage markets through indirect tax and subsidy instruments. While countries vary widely in such support, U.S. government programs are among the most extensive. The most significant program is the opportunity for U.S. taxpayers to deduct mortgage interest from their personal income taxes. The United States appears to allow the most complete deductions, while the United Kingdom—as a primary example—allows no deduction at all.[29] Other unique U.S. tax benefits include special capital-gain rules and the tax deductibility of state property taxes.

As a summary of the comparison between the role of GSEs in Europe and the United States, it is useful to consider the conclusion Coles and Hardt reached in a study published while Hardt was secretary general of the European Mortgage Federation:

> There is no national or European government agency to help lenders fund their loans. Mortgage loans have to be funded on the basis of the financial strength of banks or the intrinsic quality of the securities. EU Law (Article 87 and 88 of the EC treaty) outlaws state aid in the form of guarantees as there may be an element of competitive distortion.[30]

It is clear that the strong performance of western European housing and mortgage markets has been achieved with decidedly less government intervention than in the United States. This analysis continues by looking at two other factors that may be responsible for success in western European housing and mortgage-market performance.

Covered Bonds versus Mortgage-Backed Securitization

EUROPEAN MORTGAGE MARKETS use relatively little mortgage-backed securitization, but covered bonds are a significant factor and serve a similar function of linking bank lenders with capital-market investors. Table 4 shows the ratios of covered bonds to residential mortgages outstanding for the same set of western European countries covered in Table 1. While most of the countries use covered bonds to fund 10–20 percent of their mortgages, covered bonds dominate in three countries: Denmark (100 percent), Sweden (57 percent), and Spain (50 percent). Tests for statistical correlations indicate no significant relationships between the covered-bond use in Table 4 and the mortgage-market performance in Table 1.[31]

In comparing the U.S. and European systems, it is noteworthy that private-label MBS investors look only to the mortgage collateral to protect against credit losses whereas covered-bond investors receive a bank guarantee as well as collateral. Conversely, covered bonds are issued as a single-class obligation, whereas MBS use their multiclass structured format to allocate the primary credit risk to the most junior tranche.[32] The implication is that the

MBS system is better able to handle relatively risky mortgages by allocating the risk of the junior tranche to more knowledgeable and risk-tolerant investors. In contrast, covered bonds are generally backed by very high-quality mortgages, including the associated contractual and regulatory requirements.

A covered bond system is most effective with relatively safe underlying mortgages, whereas securitization is most valuable when the mortgages contain significant credit risk. Thus, both systems have adapted to fit the underlying mortgages with which they are associated.

Western European Mortgage Market Success: Safe Mortgages

THE FINAL COMPARISON to make between European and U.S. mortgage markets is of mortgage-contract features and underwriting standards. The United States is renowned for offering a wide menu of mortgage choice. European countries also offer a wide range of mortgage contracts, although the variation occurs more across countries than within an individual country.[33] Three key mortgage attributes have differentiated U.S. and western European mortgages:

1. Fixed-rate mortgages (FRMs) versus ARMs,

2. Prohibitions against prepayment penalties, and

3. Prohibitions against lender recourse to a borrower's nonhousing assets in default.

Fixed-Rate versus Adjustable-Rate Mortgages

HISTORICALLY, WESTERN EUROPEAN countries specialized in either FRMs or ARMs. For example, the United Kingdom has long emphasized ARMs whereas Denmark primarily used FRMs. The trend throughout Europe, however, is for countries to offer a greater menu of contract options, and both ARMs and FRMs now appear to be available in most countries. Many view the GSEs as critical for the provision of FRMs in the United States, but the facts show quite the opposite. The GSEs' MBS impose 100 percent of the interest-rate risk on third-party investors and generally allow free prepayment options for borrowers, accentuating investors' interest-rate risk. Neither of these features promotes FRMs. Indeed, the limitations of the GSEs in promoting FRMs is reflected in the fact that the U.S. ARM share has reached as much as 35 percent during at least three separate episodes over the last 15 years, while the ARM share in the European Union is about 40 percent.[34] Finally, the availability of FRMs in most western European countries—and the dominance of FRMs in several western European countries—demonstrate that GSEs are not essential for FRM contracts.

Government Regulations Prohibiting Prepayment Penalties

SOME U.S. STATES restrict the ability of residential mortgage lenders to impose prepayment penalties on their mortgage contracts. In addition, the GSEs have always resisted acquiring mortgages with prepayment penalties, in part as a mechanism to standardize their MBS. This contrasts with the U.S. market for commercial mortgages, where prepayment penalties in the form of yield maintenance or defeasance are standard. Western European residential mortgage contracts also regularly require significant prepayment penalties, very much like the penalties U.S. commercial mortgages require.[35] The absence of prepayment penalties on standard U.S. FRMs adds approximately 50 bps to the mortgage interest rate. Prepayment penalties have contributed to the superior performance of the western European mortgage markets. However, private U.S. mortgage markets would be able to provide comparably lower U.S. mortgage rates for U.S. borrowers willing to accept prepayment penalties.

Recourse and Limited Mortgage Defaults

PERHAPS THE MOST important distinction between U.S. and western European mortgage contracts is in recourse and limited mortgage defaults. In the United States, recourse varies by state; even where it is allowed, it is rarely applied.[36] This is because banks must satisfy strong U.S. consumer-protection rules before they can obtain a recourse judgment, and U.S. consumers have the option to apply for a relatively easy bankruptcy. Recourse is, therefore, not an important safeguard for U.S. mortgage investors. In contrast, recourse is standard and enforcement is firm for most western European mortgage contracts; as a result, western European lenders, borrowers, and governments act in their mutual interest to create safe mortgages.[37] Even with rapidly falling home prices, default rates on western European mortgages remain remarkably low from a U.S. perspective. Furthermore, the superior western European mortgage-market performance applies to most market indicators, as shown in Table 1.

THE LIKELY STRUCTURE AND PERFORMANCE OF A PRIVATE U.S. MORTGAGE MARKET

BY COMBINING INFORMATION from the above case studies of 15 European countries with the unique features of the U.S. housing and mortgage markets, a view of the likely structure and performance of a private U.S. mortgage market can be developed. Of course, future regulations may either facilitate or rule out certain features, so the view put forth in this chapter is necessarily conditional on how mortgage-market reform is actually implemented.

As developed earlier in this chapter, the fundamental features of a mortgage market are described by the mortgage origination, contract design and underwriting, and placement with long-term investors. Below, the chapter looks at those features—as well as possible future innovations and regulatory requirements—to describe the changes that can be expected if the United States shifts from a GSE-dominated to a private-institution-dominated mortgage market.

- **Mortgage originations.** U.S. mortgages have always been originated by private firms and banks, and this will surely continue in the absence of the GSEs.

- **Contract design and underwriting.** The absence of GSEs will immediately allow a private market to provide an expanded range of contract choices. The GSEs focused on creating a single standardized mortgage contract, the 30-year fixed payment FRM with no prepayment penalties and effectively no recourse to borrower assets beyond the housing collateral. While private lenders did create a range of alternative mortgages—including ARMs, jumbos, and so forth—they always had to compete with the subsidized GSEs.

Without the GSE obstacle, a private market will provide an extended menu: fixed-rate versus adjustable-rate, prepayment penalties or not, recourse or not, and so on. A lower mortgage rate will result when the choice benefits the lender; a higher rate will result when the choice benefits only the borrower. Borrowers will choose the contract features that are best for their specific circumstances. Of course, complete and accessible disclosures of the terms and conditions of these mortgages would be required for borrowers to make informed decisions. The Federal Reserve's July 2008 expansion of the Truth in Lending regulations already ensures a great deal of this disclosure, and a further expansion to fill in any missing parts may be necessary.[38] Informed borrowers will make good decisions as long as a competitive mortgage market provides a full menu with fair prices.

The outcome of this process will likely be a U.S. mortgage market in which mortgages are intrinsically safer, with default and foreclosure rates that more closely resemble the European markets than the recent U.S. subprime experience. Mortgage default is incredibly costly to all parties: lenders and investors face the legal costs of foreclosure and the need to sell properties under distressed conditions, borrowers lose their homes and credit ratings, and the government is called upon to fix the problem after the fact. A key virtue of a private mortgage market is that both risky and safe mortgages will be originated, but the holders of the risky contracts will pay the full price of their risk, and the holders of the safe mortgages will realize the full benefits of their safety.

- **Mortgage investors.** On the surface, the changes for mortgage investors will be minor. The GSEs hold approximately 12 percent of all U.S. whole home mortgages and MBS, and this share will be readily taken up by the depository institutions and capital-market investors. At a deeper level, however, the changes will be more substantive. The market will determine who holds the new mortgages: depositor-institution mortgage portfolios can be funded with deposits or with covered bonds, or they can be sold to third-party investors through traditional securitization. The preferred outcome will depend largely on the quality of underlying mortgages. Pools of high-quality mortgages may be retained by depository lenders and funded with either deposits or covered bonds. Pools of riskier mortgages will more likely be securitized, taking advantage of structured finance to allocate the first-loss risk among the most knowledgeable and risk-tolerant investors.

Though not always recognized, over the past 100 years of U.S.—and world—finance, the demand for virtually risk-free investments has generally exceeded readily available supply. This meant any entrepreneur able to expand the supply of AAA-rated investments would receive a large payoff. In fact, the demand for such securities was a major force leading to the creation of the senior and super-senior AAA-rated tranche of subprime MBS and collateralized debt obligation securitizations. These senior and super-senior securities turned out not to be anywhere near as safe as advertised. The high demand for AAA-rated investments persists today, perhaps more than ever. Truly high-quality mortgages could be an important part of the solution as backing for either AAA-rated covered bonds or a senior MBS tranche. The mortgage markets and the capital markets will both benefit.

- **Further features.** The re-creation of the U.S. mortgage market without the GSEs will surely motivate a variety of renewed activities and new innovations. For example, the role for private mortgage insurance (PMI) in the U.S. mortgage market could expand. Although the GSEs were a major customer for the PMI industry, modern U.S. PMI existed and expanded well before the GSEs became important. More generally, a key benefit of a private mortgage market is that the market itself will test and evaluate the proposed innovations, implement the successes, and discard the failures. And this activity will occur without imposing costs on U.S. taxpayers.

- **Regulatory requirements.** While a private mortgage market would generally operate in a safe and stable fashion, as it has in western Europe, a critical role for regulation and government oversight remains. As previously noted, the FHA and HUD programs would continue under the proposal set out in this chapter. Also, the borrower protections and full disclosures under the Truth in Lending Act and similar statutes are critical. Expanded regulatory oversight of the depository institutions in regard to all their activities as mortgage originators, servicers, investors, and issuers of covered bonds is required. There are two reasons such depository regulation is needed: (1) deficient bank regulation was a major source of the subprime crisis and must be fixed, and (2) a private mortgage market will likely channel a greater volume of mortgage lending, investing, and securitizing through the banking system. Since taxpayers backstop the banking system through government deposit insurance, their interests must be protected through aggressive regulation.

ALTERNATIVE PROPOSALS

THE NEED TO reform the U.S. mortgage markets has been recognized at least since 2008 when the full dimensions of the GSE and subprime crash became evident. For example, Federal Reserve Chairman Ben S. Bernanke provided an early call for action, including alternatives ranging from a completely private market to re-creating the GSEs.[39] The Government Accountability Office (GAO) and Congressional Budget Office (CBO) followed with similar arrays of options, including factual comments on the alternatives.[40] The long-awaited Treasury/HUD white paper and proposal was released February 12, 2011.[41]

Consistent with the premise of this volume, the Treasury/HUD white paper sets the unequivocal goal of winding down the GSEs. And consistent with the specific proposal offered in this paper, the white paper proposes to achieve this goal by lowering the conforming loan limits and raising the GSEs' guarantee fees. Furthermore, the white paper's "Option 1" is, in effect, the private-market proposal offered in this chapter. The white paper's "Option 2" is also closely aligned with the proposal of this chapter; it primarily adds the capability to expand the FHA or a similar government-guarantee program rapidly in the event of a future crisis.

The white paper's "Option 3" differs more substantially from this chapter, however. It suggests possibly offering government mortgage guarantees on a continuing basis and on a potentially wide range of mortgages. In one interpretation, this option replaces the government guarantee of the GSEs with a direct guarantee on all conforming MBS. Specific versions of similar proposals are available from Acharya, Richardson, Van Nieuwerburgh, and White; the Center for American Progress; Ellen, Tye, and Willis; and Hancock and Passmore.[42] While these plans differ in details and specificity, a composite can be summarized as follows:

- These plans anticipate that the government will set high underwriting standards for all mortgages that underlie the qualifying MBS.

- Investors in the qualifying MBS will be protected

from default losses by a mixture of private capital and government guarantees—with the government component considered essential.

- Both the private and government insurers will receive risk-based insurance premiums.

For simplicity, this structure is referred to as the "insurance proposal." It is clearly preferable to any plan that would re-create the GSEs, since for the first time the government would control the underwriting standards and be compensated for the risk it bears. The two key questions are:

1. Can the government carry out this activity effectively and efficiently?

2. Is the government's role important for a well-functioning U.S. mortgage market?

The answer to both questions is negative.

Regarding the first question, the government generally is ineffective in setting standards for its insurance programs. Government is fundamentally unable to enforce risk-based pricing—where those posing greater risks are required to pay appropriately larger premiums. Government plans almost always lead to significant subsidies, especially for the highest risks. This occurs because political pressures, understandably, make it very difficult for a government program to set high underwriting standards that exclude many higher-risk parties from the program. And once higher-risk parties are allowed into the program, the same political pressures make it very difficult to impose higher premiums on these riskier policyholders.

As a result, government insurance programs invariably have two negative effects. First, by subsidizing the riskier participants, the government actually encourages risky behavior. Second, sooner or later, the riskier pool will create large losses, and taxpayers will cover the costs. The National Flood Insurance Program provides a case study. While for many years the program appeared to break even—with premiums covering losses—it turned out that no reserves had been accumulated for a disproportionate disaster. This became clear only when the losses created by Hurricane Katrina required a taxpayer bailout on the order of $18 billion. Bank insurance provided by the Federal Deposit Insurance Corporation provides another example.[43]

With regard to the second question, government insurance simply is not needed. Most western European mortgage markets operate without government insurance, and there is no evidence this has impeded their performance. Furthermore, the United States already has two forms of mortgage insurance programs that can—and would—be expanded if needed. First, PMI already exists, including a well-structured regulatory regime. It is likely that certain classes of mortgages should be insured and that the PMI industry would provide the insurance. Second, the government's FHA program for insuring mortgages for lower-income and other socially worthy borrowers has existed since 1934, and it has never required a government bailout. The FHA program could be expanded rapidly if private markets failed to provide adequate access to the U.S. mortgage market, for example, in a future financial crisis—whether originating in the housing market or elsewhere in the economy—in which the supply of private capital to the mortgage market is disrupted. In effect, this is the Treasury/HUD white paper's Option 2.

SUMMARY AND CONCLUSIONS

THIS CHAPTER HAS developed and evaluated a proposal to reform the U.S. mortgage system along private-market principles and without any form of GSEs. The proposal would be implemented through the simple process of reducing the GSE conforming loan limit by, say, $100,000 annually, in which case the GSEs would cease to operate after about seven years. The transition process would be smooth, be anticipated by the private markets, and allow for a government reaction should it fail to proceed as expected. The proposal also advocates continuing the current FHA and HUD programs in support of lower-income families. In this form, the proposal is very similar to both Options 1 and 2 in the Treasury/HUD proposal released in a February 2011 white paper.

The primary question regarding the proposal is very direct: Will a private market provide the stability and access to mortgage credit required by U.S. homebuyers? This paper provides an affirmative answer based on two sets of evidence. First, the GSEs have played no role in originating U.S. mortgages and a relatively minor role as investors in these mortgages, so it will not be difficult for the private markets—principally depository institutions and capital-market investors—to replace them. Second, western Europe provides a very important case study of the high performance achieved by private mortgage markets in the absence of significant government interventions.

The analysis in this paper also outlines how a private U.S. mortgage market operating without GSEs likely would be structured. Mortgage-origination activity would be unchanged from the current system since originations are already carried out only by private-market entities. Similarly, mortgage investing would continue to be dominated by the two largest existing holders: depository institutions and capital-market investors. Depository institutions will continue to hold a significant number of whole mortgages in their portfolios, and capital-market investor portfolios will continue to be dominated by MBS. Covered bonds are also likely to play a more important role in the U.S. market as depository institutions fund some of their mortgage portfolios by issuing secured debt to capital-market investors. In this fashion, the market should readily absorb the 12 percent market share vacated by the departing GSEs.

The most important changes in the U.S. mortgage market are likely to occur in the types of mortgage contracts offered and in the underwriting standards imposed on borrowers. A private mortgage market is likely to provide borrowers with an expanded menu of choices, including such features as FRMs versus ARMs, contracts with or without prepayment penalties, and contracts with or without recourse to a borrower's nonhousing assets. At the same time, borrowers would face risk-based pricing: borrowers who present a higher risk to lenders or who take riskier mortgages will face appropriately higher mortgage rates. Lower-risk borrowers and contracts will be rewarded with lower mortgage rates. Given this direct incentive, borrowers overall will choose safer mortgages, thus reducing the average mortgage interest rate. Based on the western European experience, U.S. mortgage interest rates would likely fall under the proposed system, since the benefits of safer mortgages would more than offset the loss of government subsidies. In addition, the proposal would benefit U.S. taxpayers since the taxpayer costs of the GSE subsidy far exceeded its possible benefits.

NOTES

1. Dwight M. Jaffee, "The Role of the GSEs and Housing Policy in the Subprime Crisis" (testimony before the Financial Crisis Inquiry Commission, February 26, 2010), http://fcic-static.law.stanford.edu/cdn_media/fcic-testimony/2010-0227-Jaffee.pdf.
2. Government Accountability Office (GAO), "Fannie Mae and Freddie Mac: Analysis of Options for Revising the Housing Enterprises' Long-Term Structures," GAO Report 09-782, September 10, 2009, http://www.gao.gov/products/GAO-09-782.
3. "Mortgage Originations Surge in Third Quarter as Record Low Interest Rates Spur Refinancing," *Inside Mortgage Finance* 27, no. 41, October 28, 2010.
4. The FHA and GNMA reside within the U.S. Department of Housing and Urban Development (HUD) and provide direct support for the mortgage market. There are also many indirect mortgage and housing policies, the quantitatively most important of which is the federal tax deductibility of household mortgage interest payments. For surveys of the full range of government programs in support of the U.S. housing and mortgage markets, see Dwight M. Jaffee and John M. Quigley, "Housing Subsidies and Homeowners: What Role for Government-Sponsored Enterprises?" (Brookings-Wharton Papers on Urban Economics, 2007), 103–30; and Dwight M. Jaffee and John M. Quigley, "Housing Policy, Mortgage Policy, and the Federal Housing Administration," *Measuring and Managing Federal Financial Risk*, ed. Deborah Lucas (Chicago: University of Chicago Press, National Bureau of Economic Research, 2010), 97–125.

5. Fannie Mae and Freddie Mac would not be the first GSEs to lose that status. Sallie Mae, the GSE supporting the student loan market, was successfully privatized in 1996; see Michael J. Lea, "Privatizing a Government Sponsored Enterprise:Lessons from the Sallie Mae Experience" (Policy Brief 2006-PB-09, Networks Financial Institute, Indiana State University, April 2006), http://www.networksfinancialinstitute.org/Lists/Publication%20Library/Attachments/29/2006-PB-09_Lea.pdf. Although this chapter does not focus on the Federal Home Loan Bank System (FHLBS), there is merit in the recent white paper proposal by the Treasury and HUD that argues the FHLBS should be allowed to continue to provide support for the mortgage market activities of small and medium-sized U.S. banks. See U.S. Treasury and HUD, "Reforming America's Housing Finance Market: A Report to Congress," February 2011.

6. These special classes include a variety of programs in support of multifamily housing for which the GSEs played a leading role. For more details on these programs, see Ingrid Gould Ellen, John Napier Tye, and Mark A. Willis, "Improving U.S. Housing Finance through Reform of Fannie Mae and Freddie Mac: Assessing the Options," Furman Center for Real Estate and Urban Policy, New York University, May 2010.

7. U.S. Treasury and HUD, "Reforming America's Housing Finance Market."

8. Dwight M. Jaffee, "How to Privatize the Mortgage Market," *Wall Street Journal*, October 25, 2010.

9. Edward L. Glaeser and Dwight M. Jaffee, "What to Do about Fannie and Freddie?" *Economists' Voice* 3, no. 7, September 2006, http://www.bepress.com/ev/vol3/iss7/art5; Edward L. Glaeser, "When Privatization Increases Public Spending," *(Economix Blog) New York Times*, November 9, 2010, http://economix.blogs.nytimes.com/2010/11/09/when-privatization-increases-public-spending; and Dwight M. Jaffee, "The Future Role of Fannie Mae and Freddie Mac in the U.S. Mortgage Market" (paper, AEA/AREUEA meetings, Atlanta, GA, January 3, 2010), http://faculty.haas.berkeley.edu/jaffee/Papers/JaffeeGSEAtlanta.pdf.

10. Over time, this standard became automated as part of computer software maintained by both GSEs—*LoanProspector* by Freddie Mac and *Desktop Originator and Underwriter* by Fannie Mae. Using this software, a mortgage originator would know if a GSE would accept a specific pool of mortgages.

11. Life insurers were also significant and expanding home-mortgage lenders in the United States until 1970, with a market share about equal to that of commercial banks. Thrift institutions were the single largest lender group through 1970.

12. The banks in the FHLBS are also GSEs, but in this paper "GSE" refers only to Fannie Mae and Freddie Mac. As noted earlier, while the FHLBS banks are not the focus of this chapter, there is merit in allowing this system to continue

to provide support for the mortgage-market activities of small and medium U.S. banks.

13. In particular, as the GSE-retained mortgage portfolios run off, so will the debt that funded these portfolios. The investors in this debt are one example of a set of investors that could replace the GSEs as mortgage holders.

14. Brent W. Ambrose, Michael LaCour-Little, and Anthony B. Sanders, "The Effect of Conforming Loan Status on Mortgage Yield Spreads: A Loan Level Analysis," *Real Estate Economics* 32, no. 4 (2004): 541–69. Some recent press reports suggest mortgage rates could rise as much as a full percentage point, but I know of no studies that document an increase of anywhere near this amount.

15. A parallel paper by Michael Lea uses a different data set to provide a comparable survey of mortgage markets for developed countries around the world. The results garnered from the two data sets are virtually in complete concordance. See Michael Lea, "International Comparison of Mortgage Product Offerings," Research Institute for Housing America and Mortgage Bankers Association, September 2010, http://www.housingamerica.org/RIHA/RIHA/Publications/74023_10122_Research_RIHA_Lea_Report.pdf.

16. It may seem surprising that the "socialized" countries of western Europe have limited government interventions in their housing and mortgage markets. One explanation is that such interventions would likely violate the European Union prohibitions against countries using subsidies to provide unfair advantages to local agents and firms.

17. For an extensive review of housing finance in the European Union countries, see European Central Bank, "Housing Finance in the Euro Area" (Occasional Paper Series no. 101, March 2009).

18. European Mortgage Federation, *Hypostat*, 2009, European Mortgage Federation website, http://hypo.org/Content/default.asp?PageID=524.

19. Maria Conceeta Chirui and Tullio Jappelli, "Financial Market Imperfections and Home Ownership: A Comparative Study," *European Economic Review* 47 (2003): 857–75.

20. Variable mortgage rates are the only data systematically available for Europe over the required time span and for all countries; see European Mortgage Federation, *Hypostat*, for detailed definitions. The Freddie Mac one-year ARM rate was chosen as the closest equivalent for the United States.

21. Peter Neuteboom, "A Comparative Analysis of the Net Cost of a Mortgage for Homeowners in Europe," *Journal for Housing and the Built Environment* 19, no. 2 (2004): 169–86. Neuteboom has computed the net interest rate—the nominal interest rate adjusted for contractual, cost, and subsidy factors—for a range of European countries. Austria, Ireland, and Spain are the only countries for which the net interest rate is significantly higher than

the nominal rate—about 100 bps in each country. It is unclear how U.S. mortgage rates would fare under the net interest rate criterion.

22. For confirmation of the conclusion that U.S. mortgage interest rates are generally higher than those in western Europe, see European Central Bank, "Housing Finance in the Euro Area," 71.

23. Studies have noted that significant depth for a country's mortgage market requires a sound legal and accounting infrastructure. The countries in Table 1 all have such an infrastructure, but establishing this infrastructure is of fundamental importance for developing countries if they are also to create significant mortgage markets. See Veronica Cacdac Warnock and Francis E. Warnock, "Markets and Housing Finance," *Journal of Housing Economics* 17 (2008): 239–51; and Bertrand Renaud, "Mortgage Finance in Emerging Markets: Constraints on Feasible Development Paths," *Mortgage Markets Worldwide*, Danny Ben-Sharar ed. (Hoboken, NJ: Wiley, 2009), 253–88.

24. Jodie Ginsberg and Lorraine Turner, "Analysis: Irish Mortgage Arrears Manageable—for Now," Reuters, November 11, 2010, http://www.reuters.com/article/idUSTRE6AA4NJ20101111.

25. European Central Bank, "Housing Finance in the Euro Area," 73.

26. Few studies have provided quantified and institutional comparisons of mortgage systems among developed countries. For an early, unique, and book-length description of housing-finance systems in developed and developing countries around the world, see Mark Boleat, *National Housing Finance Systems: A Comparative Study* (London: Croom Helm, 1985). For country studies and a statistical comparison of the efficiency of alternative mortgage-market systems, see D. B. Diamond Jr. and Michael Lea, "Housing Finance in Developed Countries: An International Comparison of Efficiency," *Journal of Housing Research* 3 (1992), whole issue. The consulting firm Mercer Oliver Wyman has participated in two studies of the European mortgage markets; see Mercer Oliver Wyman and European Mortgage Federation, "Study on the Financial Integration of European Mortgage Markets," October 2003, http://www.hypo.org/Content/Default.asp?PageID=203; and Mercer Oliver Wyman and Mortgage Insurance Trade Association, "Risk and Funding in European Residential Mortgages: Responding to Changes in Mortgage Demand," April 15, 2011. For a recent overview of OECD housing and mortgage markets, see Cristophe André, "A Bird's Eye View of OECD Housing Markets" (OECD Economics Department Working Papers no. 746, January 28, 2010), http://www.iut.nu/Literature/2010/HousingMarket_inOECDregion_2010.pdf.

27. For good overviews of European government interventions in the mortgage markets—including subsidies, taxation, andregulation—see Lea, "International Comparison of Mortgage Product Offerings"; Mercer

Oliver Wyman and European Mortgage Federation, "Study on the Financial Integration of European Residential Mortgages"; and Mercer Oliver Wyman and Mortgage Insurance trade Association, "Risk and Funding in European Residential Mortgages."

28. Lea, "International Comparison of Mortgage Product Offerings."

29. For a detailed description of the income tax benefits afforded mortgage finance in a large number of European Union countries, see European Central Bank, "Housing Finance in the Euro Area," 84.

30. Adrian Coles and Judith Hardt, "Mortgage Markets: Why U.S. and EU Markets Are So Different," *Housing Studies* 15, no. 5 (2000): 778.

31. Covered bonds are also backed by local government loans in some of these countries, but those bonds are not included in Table 4.

32. The multiclass structured instruments also allow the interest rate risk to be distributed among those investors most tolerant of this risk.

33. For a detailed discussion of the mortgage contracts offered in a range of developed countries, see Lea, "International Comparison of Mortgage Product Offerings."

34. John Krainer, "Mortgage Choice and the Pricing of Fixed-Rate and Adjustable-Rate Mortgages," *Economic Letter*, Federal Reserve Bank of San Francisco, February 1, 2010; and European Central Bank, "Housing Finance in the Euro Area."

35. Mercer Oliver Wyman and Mortgage Insurance Trade Association, "Risk and Funding in European Residential Mortgages."

36. Andra C. Ghent and Marianna Kudlyak, "Recourse and Residential Mortgage Default: Theory and Evidence from the U.S. States" (working paper 09-10, Federal Reserve Bank of Richmond, Richmond, VA, July 7, 2009), http://www.fhfa.gov/webfiles/15051/website_ghent.pdf.

37. For a description of the mortgage-collateral rules and recourse across all western European countries, see European Mortgage Federation, "Study on the Efficiency of the Mortgage Collateral in the European Union," May 2007, http://62.102.106.72/Common/GetFile.asp?ID=5353&logonname=guest&mfd=off.

38. Federal Reserve Board of Governors, "Highlights of the Final Rule Amending Home Mortgage Provisions of Regulation Z (Truth in Lending)," news release, July 14, 2008, http://www.federalreserve.gov/newsevents/press/bcreg/regz20080714.htm.

39. Ben S. Bernanke, "The Future of Mortgage Finance in the United States" (speech; UC–Berkeley/UCLA Symposium: The Mortgage Meltdown, the Economy, and Public Policy; Berkeley, CA; October 31, 2008), http://www.federalreserve.gov/newsevents/speech/bernanke20081031a.htm.

40. Government Accountability Office, "Fannie Mae and Freddie Mac: Analysis

of the Options for Revising the Housing Enterprises' Long-Term Structures";
and Congressional Budget Office, "Fannie Mae, Freddie Mac, and the Federal
Role in the Secondary Mortgage Market," CBO Study, December 2010, http://
www.cbo.gov/ftpdocs/120xx/doc12032/12-23-FannieFreddie.pdf.

41. Treasury and HUD, "Reforming America's Housing Finance Market."

42. Viral Acharya, Matthew Richardson, Stijn Van Nieuwerburgh, and
Lawrence J. White, *Guaranteed to Fail* (Princeton: Princeton University Press,
2011); Center for American Progress, Mortgage Finance Working Group, "A
Responsible Secondary Market System for Housing Finance," July 21, 2010,
http://www.americanprogress.org/issues/2010/09/pdf/housing_finance
_slides.pdf; Ingrid Gould Ellen, John Napier Tye, and Mark A. Willis,
"Improving U.S. Housing Finance through Reform of Fannie Mae and Freddie
Mac: Assessing the Options," Furman Center for Real Estate and Urban Policy,
New York University, May 2010, http://furmancenter.org/files/publications
/Improving_US_Housing_Finance_Fannie_Mae_Freddie_Mac_9_8_10.
pdf; and Diana Hancock and Wayne Passmore, "An Analysis of Government
Guarantees and the Functioning of Asset-Backed Securities Markets" (Finance
and Economic Discussion Series No. 2010-46, Federal Reserve Board, 2010).

43. For further discussion of failed government insurance programs,
see Dwight M. Jaffee and Thomas Russell, "Should Government Provide
Catastrophe Insurance?" *The Economists' Voice* 3, no. 5 (2006): article 6,
http://www.bepress.com/ev/vol3/iss5/art6.

TWO APPROACHES TO GSE REFORM

ARNOLD KLING

THE TWO APPROACHES to housing reform offered here begin with the devil-you-know approach. This approach, which involves reviving the GSE model, has a number of advantages. It would ensure the survival of the 30-year fixed-rate mortgage. It would take advantage of the substantial organizational capital that the GSEs have accumulated with respect to standardizing mortgage lending, managing credit risk and interest-rate risk, and using computer technology to handle complexity and achieve reliability. In addition, there is a regulatory model for the GSEs, based on stress testing, that is very robust: it only failed because political leaders imposed other priorities on the GSEs that were in conflict with safety and soundness. Using the lessons learned so painfully in the recent crisis, this regulatory model can be solidified.

Any attempt to reengineer a housing-finance system with a new set of government-guaranteed entities would entail all of the risks of restoring the existing GSEs and more. Taxpayers would be exposed to similar potential hazards but with new and inexperienced organizations engaged in enterprise management and regulatory oversight.

The second option, the Jimmy Stewart banker approach, has the advantage of reducing government involvement in the mortgage market. It likely would lead to a more decentralized mortgage-finance system with a much smaller role for Wall Street, thus reviving an American tradition of smaller, independent financial institutions. It would create a playing field that is not dominated by gigantic, government-advantaged firms. It would offer politicians fewer opportunities to impose priorities on the mortgage-lending process—such as housing affordability—that produce instability and hazard. It would not set up a system in which GSE shareholders have an interest in seeking out high-risk, high-return strategies that conflict with the public interest.

The next section of this paper discusses public policy objectives that pertain to housing and the GSEs. It then describes the devil-you-know approach of restoring the GSEs with an improved regulatory structure. After that, it describes the Jimmy Stewart banker approach, in which mortgage lending might revert to an originate-and-hold model rather than rely on securitization. The conclusion explains why the second approach may be preferable.

PUBLIC POLICY OBJECTIVES

THE KEY TO successful reform in housing finance is the clarification of public policy objectives. Why does the government want to encourage home ownership? What role, if any, should subsidized mortgages play in achieving these objectives?

Vague and contradictory objectives played a large role in the catastrophes that befell Freddie Mac and Fannie Mae. Prior to the 1990s, the GSEs were chartered to purchase "investment-quality" mortgages, meaning loans with a low probability of default. However, GSE legislation enacted in 1992 explicitly included a goal of supporting "affordable housing." In issuing regulations to implement this legislation, the U.S. Department of Housing and Urban Development (HUD) set goals that led the GSEs to equate "affordable housing" with low down-payment lending or lending to borrowers with poor credit histories.[1] Thus, the "affordable-housing mission" came into conflict with the original mandate for the GSEs to back only investment-quality mortgages.

Former Treasury Secretary Lawrence Summers expressed the frustration of dealing with this lack of clarity:

> What went wrong? The illusion that the companies were doing virtuous work made it impossible to build a political case for serious regulation. When there were social failures, the companies always blamed their need to perform for the shareholders. When there were business failures, it was always the result of their social obligations. Government budget discipline was not appropriate because it was always emphasized that they were "private companies." But market discipline was nearly nonexistent given the general perception—now validated—that their debt was government backed. Little wonder

with gains privatized and losses socialized that the enterprises have gambled their way into financial catastrophe.[2]

The lack of clear public policy objectives created an opening for the executives of Fannie Mae and Freddie Mac to steamroll those in the private sector or Washington who might attempt to get in their way.[3]

Rather than employing the vague term "affordable housing," policy makers should articulate clear objectives with respect to the mortgage market. The issues include the extent to which government should subsidize mortgage credit, goals for the distribution of mortgage credit, and goals for shaping the types of loans available in the market.

Policy makers have wanted to encourage homeownership. There is a belief that owner-occupants create stable communities where properties are well maintained, and there is a concern that renting is associated with transience and property depreciation. In addition, homeownership can promote thrift. As mortgage loans amortize and house prices increase, homeowners accumulate an asset in the form of home equity.[4]

In practice, the pursuit of these goals through mortgage policy has been inefficient and even counterproductive. Subsidized mortgage credit helps drive up home prices, which attenuates the homeownership goal as higher prices put homes out of reach for the marginal household. In recent years, the frenzy of mortgage lending fueled speculative purchases, with 15 percent of mortgage loans going to owners who did not occupy the houses they were financing.[5] Moreover, the goal of encouraging thrift and asset accumulation was undermined by the proliferation of lending with low down payments, exotic mortgage instruments in which principal is not reduced over time, cash-out refinancing, and second mortgages.

There may be a valid social goal of providing assistance to some underqualified borrowers to purchase homes. However, programs to achieve this goal ought not to operate through indirect mortgage subsidies. Instead, they should be designed as on-budget subsidies. For example, the government could give underqualified borrowers grants that could be used to help make payments for the first three years of a mortgage. However, the interest rate on the mortgage should reflect its risk—as reduced by the existence of the grant—when priced in the market, rather than having the mortgage carry an artificial, subsidized rate.

Regardless of social goals, government should never again encourage the expansion of mortgage lending with low down payments. The intent of encouraging loans with low down payments was to enable households with little in savings to enter the home-purchase market and accumulate equity in their homes. However, this strategy for expanding homeownership backfired. Hundreds of thousands of these loans ended up in default. Many more homebuyers had their savings wiped out by the housing market crash—even if they continued making their mortgage payments.

Lowering the down payment tends to amplify the housing cycle. When prices are rising, people are more apt to buy with little money down, hoping to capitalize on continued appreciation. This behavior feeds the boom. Then, when prices stabilize, many of these speculative borrowers are unable to sustain their debt load, which causes distress sales and worsens the downturn. If the value of homeownership is that it fosters prudence, then speculative purchasing of homes with little or no money down is antithetical to that objective.

The issue of the distribution of mortgage credit caused much confusion. HUD issues quotas to the GSEs with respect to the income of borrowers, and those quotas were used in part to justify a foray into risky lending activities.[6] As the housing bubble inflated, the quotas were raised, forcing the GSEs to acquire more mortgages from low-income borrowers even as the ratio of median house price to median income was rising.

Another reason the GSEs undertook risky activity was to "follow the market." If they are to serve a public policy purpose of shaping the types of mortgage loans available, then GSEs should be holding fast to principles of responsible lending rather than following fashions.

Overall, GSE involvement in mortgage finance was totally out of proportion to the limited number of reasonable public policy objectives. The GSEs poorly managed the social goals for housing policy, and the ultimate risks borne by taxpayers cannot be justified.

Going forward, policy makers should clarify housing policy objectives in the following ways:

- Public policy should not seek to encourage mortgage borrowing as a means of promoting homeownership. Instead, homeownership should be presumed to embody a significant down payment and the gradual accumulation of equity.[7] Lenders that enjoy government backing—including banks and savings and loan associations—should not encourage the dissipation of home equity through nonamortizing mortgage loans, cash-out refinancing, or second mortgages.

- Public policy should not encourage lenient mortgage credit as a tool for income redistribution. Assistance for low-income households should consist of grants that are explicitly accounted for in the government budget. Government programs to help moderate-income households should be aimed at encouraging greater saving, not more borrowing. Buying a home with a low down payment involves gambling on house prices. While households gain when this gamble pays off, the overall social cost of this risk-taking far exceeds the benefit.

- To the extent that the government intervenes in the mortgage market, it should be selective in the products it supports, rather than subsidizing any and all forms of mortgage lending. In particular, policy makers should limit any subsidy to first mortgage loans for the purchase of an owner-occupied home with amortization that accumulates equity and a rate of interest that is fixed for five years or longer. Institutions that operate without government backing might choose to offer cash-out refinancing, second mortgages, loans for nonowner-occupied homes, nonamortizing loans, and short-term adjustable-rate loans, but there is no reason for government-backed agencies to be involved in these activities.

Taking a firm stand in favor of sound mortgage lending is the key to any housing-finance policy going forward. If policy makers agree that government involvement in the mortgage market should be limited to the purpose of supporting mortgage products that encourage the prudent accumulation of home equity, then it should be feasible to develop a sound mortgage-finance strategy. On the other hand, if the government's objectives for the mortgage market remain broad and poorly specified, any approach to reforming housing finance is likely to fail.

THE DEVIL-YOU-KNOW

BEFORE WE BURY Freddie Mac and Fannie Mae, we should praise them. As tools for making capital available for mortgage lending, the GSEs were efficient. Mortgage rates in the market for loans eligible for sale to the GSEs were typically 0.25 to 0.50 percent below those on comparable loans in the "jumbo" market—the market for mortgage amounts above the limit set for the GSEs by Congress.[8] This suggests that the GSEs were effective at funneling savings—including capital from overseas—into the U.S. mortgage market.

The GSEs' risk-management strategies and systems are very sophisticated, well-developed, and sound. These systems failed largely due to the pressure applied by political leaders to provide lenient, subsidized mortgage credit that fuelled an unsustainable expansion of speculative home buying.

To be able to channel capital from around the world into loans to individual American households to buy homes, the GSEs had to create standards for mortgage underwriting and processing. This standardization is a success story.

Mortgage underwriting is subject to the classic statistical problem of type I and type II error. Type I error is the approval of a mortgage for a borrower who subsequently defaults. This error imposes a large cost on the borrower and the lender. Type II error is the failure to approve a mortgage for a borrower who would have repaid the loan as scheduled. This error causes both the lender and the borrower to miss out on the opportunity for a mutually beneficial transaction.

Political leaders often seem unable to grasp these elementary concepts. Before the financial crisis, politicians complained about mortgage borrowers who were being turned down for loans. Implicitly, the politicians were unwilling to forgive type II errors. On the other hand, after the crisis, legislative language was proposed to forbid mortgage lenders from making loans to borrowers who could not repay, in effect trying to outlaw type I errors.

This political intervention was unwarranted and only served to exacerbate the housing cycle. During a boom, type I errors are forgiven by rising house prices that insulate lenders from risk, so it is easy for politicians to complain that too many mortgage applicants are being turned down. On the other hand, in the wake of a crash, threatening to criminalize type I errors will take away lenders' willingness to absorb risk at the time when the market needs this most.

It is unrealistic to expect to eliminate either type of error completely. Underwriting already attempts to cut down on both types of errors as much as possible. Over the last several decades, the GSEs have continually improved the accuracy of underwriting decisions, making it possible to commit fewer type II errors without adding to the risk of type I errors. Furthermore, the GSEs' promulgation of standards and automation technology has lowered the administrative costs involved in mortgage underwriting.

The GSEs have also developed a number of risk-management tools for addressing the moral hazard associated with the process of originating mortgage loans for sale to third parties. The GSEs implement quality-control audits of lenders who sell loans, and they require lenders to buy back loans that do not fall within underwriting parameters or that lack proper documentation. They set minimum capital standards for sellers to ensure that originators can, in fact, stand behind the loans they sell. The GSEs issue guidelines and training manuals to foster compliance with standards.

Additionally, the GSEs use risk-based pricing, loss reserving, and capital policies. This means that for loans with lower down payments or other characteristics that add to risk, the GSEs charge higher interest rates, set aside more reserves to cover potential losses, and maintain a larger capital base. Furthermore, the capital base is calibrated to withstand a severe stress test. At one time, the stress test was patterned after the experience of collapsing home values during the Great Depression. Subsequently, the stress test was modified to be patterned after large regional downturns during the postwar period.

Over the past decade, many critics of the GSEs warned that their large size and high leverage posed a risk to taxpayers. However, these critics tended to see interest-rate risk as the primary threat.⁹ Rather than sell mortgage securities to other institutions, the GSEs increasingly held securities in their own portfolios, financed by debt. This behavior creates a risk of maturity mismatch. If the average maturity of mortgage security assets in your portfolio is 20 years and the average maturity of your debt is five years, then rising interest rates can cause a significant loss in the portfolio's overall market value. Given the high ratio of assets to capital at these enterprises, the result could be catastrophic losses. This sort of loss plagued the savings-and-loan industry in the 1970s and early 1980s. In fact, Fannie Mae suffered losses in that period and technically may have been bankrupt.¹⁰ (Freddie Mac held a negligible portfolio in that period.)

Taking away the GSEs' power to hold mortgages in portfolio might be proposed with the intent of insulating taxpayers from a blow-up should Freddie or Fannie fail to carefully manage interest-rate risk. However, bear in mind that whatever interest-rate risk the GSEs are not taking will be borne elsewhere. Having the interest-rate risk management visible within the GSEs may be preferable to not knowing where or how interest-rate risk is being managed. With many of the nation's assets currently concentrated in the largest institutions, there is a good chance that—if interest-rate risk causes problems—one or more "too-big-to-fail" banks will be affected. Ultimately, taxpayers' exposure could be just as great or greater than if the GSEs' portfolio business had been left alone.

It is also worth pointing out that the taxpayers have not suffered from any failure of interest-rate risk management by the GSEs. Given this history, any call to restrict their operations to credit guarantees would seem perverse. It would get them out of the business that has caused no trouble while keeping them in the business that blew up in the crisis. Interest-rate risk was not a factor in the GSEs' collapse; they had to be bailed out because of credit losses. In fact, the GSEs have developed effective mechanisms for adjusting their portfolios to remain hedged with respect to the level and volatility of interest rates. Their interest-rate positions also are subjected to severe stress tests—which analyze the effect of hypothetical increases or decreases in market interest rates—to determine capital standards. This approach to managing interest-rate risk is as sound as could be hoped for.

With all of these mechanisms in place, why did the GSEs absorb such large losses that they had to be taken into conservatorship in 2008? Narrowly speaking, there appear to be two reasons. One reason is that their capital was overstated because they counted items such as tax-loss carryforwards as capital. These items did not actually constitute part of an asset base that could absorb losses, which is the purpose of capital. Another reason is that as the GSEs strayed far from the investment-quality lending (meaning mortgages with significant down payments and other risk-reducing characteristics) that was their original purpose, they failed to assess the impact of these higher-risk loans on capital needs under a stress scenario.

The agency that regulated the GSEs, known at the time as the Office of Federal Housing Enterprise Oversight (OFHEO), was derelict in executing its authority. Critics have correctly pointed out that OFHEO was structured as an arm of HUD rather than the Department of the Treasury. HUD's primary missions are to promote better housing and expand homeownership, and it was pressing the GSEs to meet affordable housing goals that conflicted with the GSEs' objective of maintaining safety and soundness in mortgage lending.

In view of this past experience, the devil-you-know approach should consist of the following elements:

- Return the GSEs to shareholder-owned status but with the government assuring investors that the firms will not be permitted to fail. Taxpayer protection would be strengthened through tighter regulation focused on maintaining the safety and soundness of the GSEs. Executing this plan probably requires wiping out existing shareholders, creating a "bad bank" to hold the securities backed by low-quality mortgages, and capitalizing both GSEs with new initial public offerings.

- Place responsibility for regulatory oversight of the GSEs under the Treasury, with a mandate to focus solely on the safety and soundness of the GSEs. The stress-test approach should be constantly improved. Above all, capital standards should be enforced, and only capital that can absorb losses should be counted.

- Abandon the practice of assigning affordable housing goals to the GSEs. Instead of creating incentives for the GSEs to undertake risky lending, the mandate to purchase only investment-quality loans should be reiterated and strengthened. The devil-you-know strategy, as envisioned here, would limit the GSEs to supporting long-term fixed-rate mortgages for well-qualified borrowers. It would not involve the GSEs in goals to expand homeownership to borrowers with inadequate income, assets, or credit scores.

- Restate the GSEs' core mission. The GSEs' purpose should be to provide long-term, fixed-rate mortgage loans to clearly qualified borrowers who make sizable down payments. A down payment of 20 percent—or 10 percent if supplemented with private mortgage insurance—was once standard and ought to become standard again. More exotic mortgage instruments might be provided by fully private lenders, but the GSEs do not need to support that market. Public policy goals to expand homeownership should be pursued through explicit, on-budget subsidies, not through cross-subsidization mandated by quotas imposed on the GSEs.

- Restrict GSEs' financial activities. The GSEs should continue to be able to hold portfolios and manage interest-rate risk, subject to capital and regulatory requirements. However, the Treasury should prevent and penalize any attempts by the GSEs to exploit their low borrowing costs by engaging in hedge-fund-like activities or other financial strategies not essential to the mortgage-securities business.

- Create a standardized national property-recording database. County recording offices use idiosyncratic documents and are highly dependent on paper. This is incompatible with the high-speed computerized trading of mortgage securities, with the result that many foreclosure notices issued in recent years have been challenged on legal grounds. To avoid a repeat of the current foreclosure mess and ensure clear property records moving forward, an agency should be created to replace local property recording offices with a definitive, standardized national database. This idea is probably wise regardless of what happens to the GSEs, but it is particularly important if securitization continues to play an important role in mortgage finance. With traditional mortgage lending, where the loan is held by the originating institution until it is repaid, the older forms of record-keeping are not much of a problem. However, with securitization, where the ownership of a mortgage can go whizzing around the globe in seconds, only a modernized record-keeping system can prevent legal tangles.

The main social benefit of the devil-you-know strategy is that it would help maintain a stable mortgage market, one dominated by the 30-year fixed-rate mortgage with a reasonable down payment.[11] Given the adverse experience that the United States has had with other mortgage instruments, both during the Great Depression and the recent crisis, the dominance of such mortgages would provide comfort and reassurance to homeowners. Note, however, that many other countries, such as Canada, have achieved high rates of homeownership with shorter-term mortgage products.

Offsetting this benefit would be the risk that the GSEs would once again fail, imposing further costs on taxpayers. However, such a risk is likely to exist under any arrangement in which the government tries to channel funds into lending to support the 30-year fixed-rate mortgage. There are not many institutions or individuals willing to tie up funds for an uncertain period of up to 30 years. True, there are pension funds and insurance companies with a need for long-term assets. However, their appetite for 30-year mortgages is not likely to be sufficient to sustain a lending volume comparable to that supported by the GSEs. To be issued in large volume, 30-year mortgages must have a funding source that offers greater liquidity, meaning that investors can get out of their positions well before the 30-year final maturity date. That, in turn, requires funding instruments that are tradable. If the value of the underlying collateral and/or viability of the institution must be assessed each time the instrument is traded, the resulting transaction costs will be prohibitively high. Thus, to make mortgage securities liquid, it is almost certain that a government guarantee will have to be inserted somewhere in the process.

Reliance on a government guarantee to help channel funds into long-term, fixed-rate mortgages is one flaw in the devil-you-know approach, because regulatory controls on risk taking tend to degrade over time. There are two sources of weakness: one financial and one political. The financial threat comes from innovation. The financial system naturally evolves mechanisms that increase the profits to be gained by exploiting a guarantee. Risk naturally flows in the direction of guarantee-backed firms. The political weakness is that regulated firms have an incentive to lobby to create opportunities to exploit guarantees. Freddie Mac and Fannie Mae were notoriously powerful in the political realm. When Treasury Secretary Henry Paulson put the GSEs under conservatorship, ending their lobbying was a high priority. There is a legitimate fear that if we return to the status quo ante, the GSEs will gradually regain their formidable political prowess. Political power in turn could be used to press for expanded opportunities for risk taking that increase the perils faced by taxpayers.

If there is bound to be a government guarantee in any event, then the challenge of protecting taxpayers from risks is going to require a regulatory mechanism. Mechanisms such as the Basel international bank capital standards or the systems used to safeguard the Federal Deposit Insurance Corporation (FDIC) and the Pension Benefit Guaranty Corporation have not performed so well that they offer an attractive alternative. Other regulatory mechanisms, such as those proposed by the Obama administration, are unproven.[12]

Given the limited options, the GSE approach offers a reasonable combination of theoretical justification and promising past performance. It is true that the system cracked due to extreme stresses and the weakness of regulatory oversight resulting from its placement under HUD. However, if the GSEs have learned their lessons from these failures, taxpayer protections can be fairly robust. The shareholder-owned structure gives the GSEs an incentive to adopt internal controls to maintain franchise value. The presence of a focused regulator using capital requirements based on stress tests forces the shareholders to have sufficient "skin in the game" that management will pay close attention to risk.

Attempting to channel funds to 30-year fixed-rate mortgages through a new entity or set of entities presumably would require the insertion of a government guarantee at some point. This strategy would trade the devil we know for the devil we don't know. We do not know what new regulatory difficulties would be posed by a different institutional structure with an embedded guarantee. However, there is little reason to expect that a new and untried regulatory mechanism will be impregnable in theory and even less reason to be confident that it will work as intended in practice.

One of the most important bulwarks that the GSEs provide against catastrophic failure is their stock of organizational capital. Their staff and computer systems have embedded knowledge relevant to solving the many problems associated with linking the capital markets to the mortgage market. Creating a new institutional structure would require at least some of this knowledge to be reinvented, imposing considerable costs—and risks—on the system.

Overall, the devil-you-know strategy seems to be the least problematic way to maintain the channels of funding between the capital markets and long-term, fixed-rate mortgages for well-qualified home buyers. The benefit of keeping interest rates low on 30-year fixed-rate mortgages may not be large when compared with the costs and trauma of the recent crisis and bailouts.[13]

THE JIMMY STEWART BANKER APPROACH

MORTGAGE LOANS USED to be made by local deposit-taking institutions, which held the loans they made. When a borrower was late with payments, the bank had local knowledge that could be used to decide the appropriate course of action. If that course of action was foreclosure, the information in the county recording office would show that the bank was the legal holder of the mortgage note and could move toward taking possession of the property.

What I call the Jimmy Stewart banker approach would require the government to exit the mortgage guarantee business. The GSEs would be gradually phased out by reducing each year, over a period of three to five years, the upper limits on the loan amounts they can purchase. At the end of this phasing-out period, their loan purchases would cease altogether.[14] As the GSEs were phased out, they would be replaced by whatever emerged in the market. One cannot predict with certainty what would evolve, but one likely scenario is that local banks would revert to the practice of originating and holding mortgages (hence the name of this approach). Another possible outcome is that the private securitization market could revive. This outcome is unlikely, however, because the agency ratings that were the key to the private mortgage-securities market have lost credibility. Another possible outcome would be the emergence of a small number of dominant national mortgage lenders able to raise capital both domestically and internationally. These would be private analogues to the GSEs. This scenario is also unlikely to occur because memories of the financial crisis will make money managers reluctant to offer low-cost financing to such enterprises.

Jimmy Stewart banks would probably offer mortgages for shorter terms than the 30-year fixed-rate mortgage that has been the standard in the United States for many years, but which is less common in most other countries. For example, the standard in Canada is a five-year rollover mortgage, in which amortization takes place on a 30-year schedule but the interest rate adjusts every five years.[15]

There are other possible outcomes. Banks might find that the interest-rate swap market or the market for covered bonds—bonds issued with mortgages as collateral—is deep enough to allow them to issue 30-year fixed-rate mortgages while laying off the interest-rate risk. However, something like the five-year rollover mortgage would likely dominate in the absence of government intervention because the regulatory environment in the United States no longer encourages depository institutions to have large maturity mismatches.

Until 1980, interest rates on deposits were regulated, and neither capital requirements nor deposit insurance premiums were calibrated to risk. In this environment, depository institutions had stable funding costs and could engage in maturity mismatching without any checks. Protected by insurance, depositors had no reason to be concerned with the institution's asset-liability strategies. The absence of risk-based capital or deposit insurance premiums left banks and thrift institutions free to try to earn the spread between regulated deposit interest rates and long-term mortgage rates.

The increase in inflation in the 1970s left many thrift institutions bankrupt. Their insolvency was disguised by historical accounting that did not recognize the losses embedded in their holdings of long-term mortgage assets.[16] However, as the 1980s wore on, the weaknesses in the thrifts' balance sheets were exposed. Many closed, and their depositors were bailed out at taxpayers' expense in what became known as the savings and loan (S&L) crisis.

The S&L crisis yielded a number of important lessons. One lesson is that regulators must be able to assess the true financial condition of depository institutions rather than allow insolvency to be disguised by historical-cost accounting. Another lesson is that deposit insurance premiums and capital requirements have to be adjusted for risk, including the interest-rate risk that depository institutions take when they fund long-term assets with deposits. Requiring higher deposit insurance premiums and imposing higher capital requirements for greater risk would make it more expensive for depository institutions to offer long-term, fixed-rate mortgages.

By 1990, the S&L industry had shrunk drastically. Over the next 20 years, the main funding instrument for long-term, fixed-rate mortgages became callable debt issued by the GSEs. The call provisions enabled the GSEs to hedge much of the risk embedded in prepayment options. That is, suppose that a mortgage borrower obtains an 8 percent, 30-year loan, and the GSE finances it by issuing 20-year bonds at an interest rate of 6.5 percent. Two years later, it might be the case that rates have fallen, with mortgage rates at 5.5 percent and bonds at 4.0 percent. In that case, borrowers will refinance at the lower rate, and if the GSE has failed to hedge against this risk, it will retain the 6.5-percent bond as a liability while having only the 5.5-percent mortgage as an asset. If the 20-year bond is callable in five years, the GSEs' exposure to prepayment risk is greatly reduced, because when interest rates fall and borrowers refinance, the GSE also can refinance by exercising the option to call the bond.

For the 30-year fixed-rate mortgage to remain attractively priced in the Jimmy Stewart banker scenario, mortgage lenders would have to be able to issue callable debt without paying a large premium over Treasury interest rates. This is unlikely. Small depository institutions lack the name recognition and market credibility to tap into important sources of funds, particularly from foreign investors. In addition, their long-term debt lacks explicit government backing—unlike their deposits, which are insured—and presumably would not carry any implicit guarantee. Thus, their debt would be unlikely to enjoy the AAA ratings that accrued to the GSEs.

In short, depository institutions would appear to lack access to low-cost, long-term funding. Relying on deposits to fund long-term, fixed-rate mortgages would, under prudent regulation, impose on these institutions substantial costs in the form of deposit-insurance premiums and capital requirements. On the other hand, attempting to match funding by tapping the long-term debt market would be more expensive than it is for the GSEs, with their worldwide recognition and government backing.

Thus, as the GSEs are phased out, a mortgage finance system would likely emerge in which mortgage loans are bought and held by depository institutions. These loans will have a 30-year amortization schedule, but the interest rate will adjust about every five years. Thirty-year fixed-rate loans will continue to be available, but at an interest-rate premium that is high enough that their market share will be much less than is the case today. This modest restructuring of mortgage credit, with more five-year adjustable-rate mortgages and fewer 30-year fixed-rate mortgages, is likely to prove benign. As noted, many other countries have done well with mortgages whose rates stay fixed for shorter periods than 30 years.

With lending decisions made by local depository institutions, mortgage finance can arrive at a better mix of rules and judgment. We are much less likely to see an outbreak of the collective insanity that infected the housing-finance system from 2003 through 2007. Under that system, a demand for mortgage-backed securities emerged that was so perversely high that mortgage originators lost any incentive to adhere to sensible underwriting standards.

One adverse consequence of a mortgage-finance system that relies on securitization carried out by entities backed by the government is that it fosters extreme concentrations in finance. A high degree of financial concentration is typical in Europe and Asia, but the United States has a longstanding tradition of preferring a more decentralized financial system. Our fear has been that large banks form a symbiotic relationship with political forces, which makes for corporatism or "crony capitalism." When finance is concentrated, government tends to become heavily involved in the allocation of capital—to the detriment of smaller entrepreneurs who lack political connections. The percentage of assets controlled by the nation's largest financial institutions was much greater during the era of securitization than was the case when S&L associations were a major factor in mortgage lending.

The problems of crony capitalism were evident with the GSEs, which were notorious for heavy-handed lobbying efforts and hiring executives with strong political connections.[17] By the same token, the market allocation of capital was heavily compromised as politicians conferred advantages on the GSEs that gave them market dominance while pressuring them to make financial decisions based on political considerations, most notably the affordable housing goals.[18]

Securitization also greatly increased the role in mortgage finance of a few Wall Street firms. These firms developed a number of financial strategies that, while profitable in the short run, exposed their companies to catastrophic risks. The 2010 Dodd-Frank financial reform bill embodies a number of regulatory mechanisms intended to prevent a recurrence of this risk exposure. However, many economists familiar with financial regulatory history are skeptical that these mechanisms will work for very long, believing instead that there is more safety in reverting to a simpler financial process that is less dependent on a few large firms.[19]

For implementing the Jimmy Stewart banker approach, the following considerations should be kept in mind:

- Regulators should monitor the distribution of interest-rate risk. They should not allow it to become concentrated in ways that put the FDIC at risk. This means banks should not be permitted to fund long-term, fixed-rate mortgages with short-term deposits without paying a stiff premium in the form of higher costs for deposit insurance or higher capital requirements. Also, to the extent that banks engage in hedging strategies that involve counterparties, regulators will need to verify the soundness of the strategies and of the counterparties. Regulators should conduct regular stress-test simulations of alternative interest-rate scenarios with respect to individual insured institutions as well as with respect to the entire system, including counterparties.

- As in the devil-you-know approach, Congress should back away from attempts to expand homeownership through lenient mortgage credit with low down payments. As discussed earlier, any housing subsidies should be on budget, in forms such as grants to assist households in making mortgage payments early in the life of the loan.

- With less government effort to steer funding toward mortgage finance, we should be prepared to see mortgage borrowing scaled back, as borrowers and lenders undertake transactions that reflect the true price of credit risk. Down payments should tend to be larger than they have been in recent years, and house-price increases should be more restrained.

This shift away from high-leverage housing finance should be considered a benefit of the Jimmy Stewart banker approach rather than a cost. With less of the world's capital siphoned into driving up house prices and leverage in the United States, more funds will be available for other productive investment projects. Such a change should also facilitate what many experts at the International Monetary Fund and elsewhere see as a long-needed adjustment in international capital flows, with the United States moderating its absorption of foreign capital and reducing its trade deficit.[20]

CONCLUSION

THE BEST APPROACH to GSE reform would be to phase out the GSEs over a period of three to five years and allow alternative channels of mortgage finance to evolve. Regulators should pay attention to this evolution to ensure that interest-rate risk does not become inappropriately concentrated—with particular concern for protecting the FDIC, which would be vulnerable if banks were to take on significant interest-rate risk as the insurer of deposits.

The basic approach to phasing out the GSEs would be to gradually reduce the ceilings on the loan amounts they can securitize. For example, if these limits were lowered by 20 percent per year, then after five years the GSEs could no longer securitize loans.

However, I would advocate eliminating some GSE activities much sooner. For example, within six months, they should stop purchasing loans for non-owner-occupied homes (including multifamily homes), cash-out refinances, and adjustable-rate mortgages. Their purchases of loans with down payments of less than 20 percent should be capped, either in dollar terms or as a percentage of loans purchased, and these caps should fall to zero within three years.

As the market evolves, it is possible—if not likely—that the interest rate on 30-year fixed-rate mortgages will rise in relation to other interest rates. This increase is likely to reduce household leverage in the housing market, and it is likely to induce many home purchasers to shift toward variable-rate instruments, such as a five-year adjustable-rate mortgage.

A GSE phase-out would help to avoid a resurgence of a financial system that became both overly concentrated and overly enmeshed in political cronyism. It would make it easier for the United States to return to its tradition of decentralized, varied financial institutions.

One concern with phasing out the GSEs is that it would put upward pressure on mortgage interest rates and consequently put downward pressure on home prices. If boosting home prices is a concern, it would be better for the government to offer a direct subsidy for home purchases than to keep the GSEs in place indefinitely. Such a subsidy to home purchases is not warranted. However, the indirect subsidy implied by keeping the GSEs at their current level of involvement in the mortgage market is even less warranted.

If the possibilities of a reduced supply of mortgage funds and a rise in the relative cost of the 30-year fixed-rate mortgage are too unpalatable to contemplate, then it would be better to restore the GSEs to their previous status rather than create a new and different structure with government backing. The GSE model can be fixed by giving their regulator an unambiguous focus on their safety and soundness mission. The regulator should insulate the GSEs from pressures to subsidize risky lending and reinstate and tighten their charter restrictions against purchasing loans with low down payments.

The worst option would be to create a new government-backed system to channel funds into mortgages. Such an approach would necessarily involve the GSE model's worst features, namely the close relationship between politics and mortgage finance, the unnatural concentration of the mortgage industry, and the inevitable deterioration of policy makers' ability to contain or correctly price risk. At the same time, a new approach would impose a steep learning curve on both the new entities and their regulators, saddling taxpayers with unnecessarily high and uncertain costs.

NOTES

1. For further documentation of the deterioration of loan quality at the GSEs, see Edward Pinto, *Government Housing Policies in the Lead-up to the Financial Crisis: A Forensic Study* (Washington, DC: American Enterprise Institute, 2010), http://papers.ssrn.com/sol3/papers.cfm?abstract_id=1675959.

2. Lawrence Summers, "You Want Creative Capitalism? Try This," *Creative Capitalism: A Conversation with Bill Gates, Warren Buffett, and Other Economic Leaders*, ed. Michael Kinsley (New York: Simon and Schuster, 2008), 196.

3. Bethany McLean and Joe Nocera, *All the Devils Are Here* (New York: Portfolio/Penguin, 2010). For example, on p. 17, "How did Fannie Mae persuade Pierce to rule in its favor? Not by sweet-talking, that's for sure; Maxwell had an iron fist inside that velvet glove of his. 'We essentially gutted some of HUD's control over us in a bill that passed the House housing subcommittee,' Maloni says today. In that bill, HUD's ability to approve new programs was revoked. HUD went to Fannie, and essentially pleaded for mercy. 'In return for asking the Congress to drop the provision, HUD approved Fannie as issuers,' says Maloni. Maloni also called Lou Nevins and told him that if Salomon didn't back off, Fannie wouldn't do business with the bank anymore. . . . This was a major threat. 'It's like the post office saying we won't deliver your mail!' Nevins says. He remembers thinking to himself, 'If they get away with this, there won't be a private company in the world that will stand up to them.'"

4. With a fixed-rate, level-payment mortgage, equity accumulates as long as house prices rise, even if they rise more slowly than the overall rate of inflation.

5. Robert B. Avery, Kenneth P. Brevoort, and Glenn B. Canner, "The 2006 HMDA Data," *Federal Reserve Bulletin*, December 2007, A73–A109.

6. Pinto, "Government Housing Policies."

7. Twenty years ago, a 20 percent down payment was standard for loans purchased by the GSEs, with down payments permitted between 10 and 20 percent provided the borrower also obtained private mortgage insurance.

8. Some estimates of the effect of the GSEs are less generous, suggesting a differential of only about 0.15 percentage points, with about half of that

coming from the GSEs funding advantages. See S. Wayne Passmore, Shane M. Sherlund, and Gillian Burgess, "The Effect of Housing Government-Sponsored Enterprises on Mortgage Rates," FEDS working paper No. 2005-06, January 2005, http://papers.ssrn.com/sol3/papers.cfm?abstract_id=658263. See also Congressional Budget Office, "Assessing the Public Costs and Benefits of Fannie Mae and Freddie Mac," May 1996, http://www.cbo.gov/ftpdocs/0xx/doc13/Fanfred.pdf.

9. Dwight M. Jaffee, "The Interest Rate Risk of Fannie Mae and Freddie Mac," *Journal of Financial Services Research* 24 (2003):1, 5–29.

10. According to the Congressional Budget Office study previously cited, "By the early 1980s, the market value of Fannie Mae's mortgages was $10 billion less than its outstanding debt."

11. I would argue that, prior to their foray into nontraditional mortgages, the GSEs *were* a stabilizing force in the mortgage market. Thus, if properly regulated, they could once again be a stabilizing force.

12. US Department of the Treasury and the US Department of Housing and Urban Development, *Reforming America's Housing Finance Market, Report to Congress*, 112 Cong., 1st sess. (Washington, DC, 2011), http://portal.hud.gov/hudportal/documents/huddoc?id=housingfinmarketreform.pdf

13. Anthony B. Sanders and Michael Lea, "Do We Need the 30-Year Fixed-Rate Mortgage?" (working paper, Mercatus Center at George Mason University, Arlington, VA, March 2011), http://mercatus.org/sites/default/files/publication/Do%20We%20Need%2030yr%20FRM.Sanders.3.14.11.pdf.

14. In addition, Federal Housing Administration (FHA) and U.S. Federal Department of Veterans Affairs (VA) mortgage loans would be replaced by grants to eligible homebuyers. These grants would be used to make mortgage payments in the first years of the mortgage. However, changes to FHA and VA mortgages can be addressed separately from the phasing out of the GSEs.

15. Donald R. Lessard, "Roll-over Mortgages in Canada," *New Mortgage Designs for Stable Housing in an Inflationary Environment*, Federal Reserve Bank of Boston Conference, vol. 14 (January 1975): 131–41, http://www.bos.frb.org/economic/conf/conf14/conf14g.pdf.

16. Elijah Brewer III, "Full-Blown Crisis, Half-Measure Cure," *Economic Perspectives*, Chicago Fed (November/December 1989), http://www.chicagofed.org/digital_assets/publications/economic_perspectives/1989/ep_nov_dec1989_part1_brewer.pdf.

17. Russell Roberts, *Gambling with Other People's Money: How Perverted Incentives Caused the Financial Crisis* (Arlington, VA: Mercatus Center at George Mason University, 2010), http://mercatus.org/sites/default/files/publication/RUSS-final.pdf.

18. Arnold Kling, *Not What They Had in Mind: A History of Policies That*

Produced the Financial Crisis of 2008 (Arlington, VA: Mercatus Center at George Mason University, 2009), http://mercatus.org/sites/default/files/publication/NotWhatTheyHadInMind%281%29.pdf.

19. See, for example, James Kwak, "Who Needs Big Banks?" *The Baseline Scenario*, October 12, 2009, http://baselinescenario.com/2009/10/12/who-needs-big-banks; Simon Johnson, "Big Sticks for US Banks," *Prospect Magazine*, July 21, 2010; and Simon Johnson, "Ending 'Too Big to Fail,'" *Economix Blog* (*New York Times*), April 8, 2010, http://economix.blogs.nytimes.com/2010/04/08/ending-too-big-to-fail.

20. See for example Martin S. Feldstein, "Resolving the Global Imbalance: The Dollar and the U.S. Saving Rate," *Journal of Economic Perspectives*, vol. 22, no. 3, Summer 2008, 113–25; Olivier J. Blanchard and Gian Maria Milesi-Ferreti, "Global Balances: In Midstream?" CEPR Discussion Paper No. DP7693, February 2010; and Maurice Obtfeld and Kenneth Rogoff, "Global Imbalances and the Financial Crisis: Products of Common Causes," CEPR Discussion Paper No. DP7606, December 2009.

A NEW HOUSING FINANCE SYSTEM FOR THE UNITED STATES

PETER J. WALLISON

IMPLICIT IN MOST of the proposals for reforming the U.S. housing finance system is the idea that mortgage-backed securities (MBS) backed by U.S. mortgages cannot be sold unless they are issued by a government-sponsored enterprise (GSE) or a U.S. government agency, or are otherwise guaranteed by the U.S. government. In this paper, I endeavor to show that continuing U.S. government involvement in the housing-finance system will inevitably involve serious losses for taxpayers and that the U.S. housing- finance system could function well without GSEs or any other form of government financial support simply by ensuring that only good quality mortgages are allowed to enter the securitization system. To demonstrate these points, it is necessary to consider the history of government financial support for housing and the costs of that government involvement.

U.S. GOVERNMENT FINANCIAL SUPPORT FOR HOUSING

THE U.S. GOVERNMENT'S involvement in housing finance began in 1934 with the creation of the Federal Housing

Administration (FHA), which had authority to insure mortgages for up to 100 percent of the loan amount. At the time, there was not a national market for mortgages, and there were many local and regional differences in mortgage terms and low loan-to-value (LTV) ratios of 50–60 percent. Fewer than 44 percent of Americans owned their own homes. Mortgage terms tended to be relatively short with bullet payments at the end. If a mortgage could not be refinanced at the end of its term—and many during the Great Depression could not be—it was foreclosed. The purpose of the FHA was to overcome the reluctance of banks and others to make mortgage loans during this period. Over time, the FHA acquired a major role in standardizing mortgage terms, increasing acceptable LTV ratios to approximately 80 percent, and encouraging the development of mortgages that amortized over multiyear periods.[1]

The FHA was able to overcome lenders' reluctance to make long-term mortgage loans, but it could not provide them with the necessary liquidity. That role fell to the Federal National Mortgage Association (better known as Fannie Mae), originally chartered in 1938 to buy mortgages that had been FHA insured. By purchasing these loans, Fannie Mae provided banks and other mortgage originators with the liquidity to make more mortgages and, thus, to finance the growth of homeownership and the U.S. housing industry. By 1950, the homeownership rate in the United States had risen to 50 percent.[2]

Savings and Loan Associations

DURING THE DEPRESSION era, Congress also created the legal structure for a system of federal savings and loan associations (S&Ls), depository institutions limited to making loans for residential housing. Under a Federal Reserve rule known as Regulation Q, deposit interest rates had been capped since 1934. In 1966, to give the S&Ls an advantage over banks in competing for deposits—and to give a financial preference to housing—the Federal Reserve adjusted the cap so S&Ls could pay one-quarter point more than banks on their deposits. This change created rapid growth in the S&L industry, which quadrupled in size between 1966 and 1979. When the rise of money-market mutual funds made it impossible for the federal government to continue to control deposit interest rates, Congress authorized the removal of deposit interest-rate caps in the Monetary Control Act of 1980.[3] With the elimination of these rate restrictions, S&Ls holding low-interest-rate, 30-year mortgages became exposed to much higher market rates for their deposits, and large portions of the industry became insolvent. The losses far exceeded the amount in the S&L insurance fund, and the taxpayers eventually absorbed a loss estimated at approximately $150 billion.

Government-Sponsored Enterprises

IN 1968, FOR budgetary reasons, Fannie Mae was "privatized" in the sense that it was allowed to sell its equity shares to the public. Privatization removed it from the federal budget, but Fannie retained sufficient ties to the government—including a congressional charter and a mission to establish and maintain a secondary market in mortgages—such that it became a quasi-public, quasi-private company, a GSE. In 1970, Congress chartered an identical GSE, Freddie Mac, primarily to provide liquidity to the S&L industry in the way Fannie provided liquidity to banks, and Congress authorized both GSEs to buy conventional mortgages in addition to those insured by the FHA or other government agencies. The congressional charters of both GSEs required that they purchase only mortgages that would be acceptable investments for institutional investors.[4]

In 1992, Congress enacted Title XIII of the Housing and Community Development Act of 1992 (the GSE Act), legislation intended to give low- and moderate-income borrowers better access to mortgage credit through Fannie Mae and Freddie Mac.[5] The act authorized the U.S. Department of Housing and Urban Development (HUD) to establish affordable-housing goals for the GSEs. These goals, which were increased substantially during the Clinton and George W. Bush administrations, required a certain percentage of all the loans Fannie and Freddie bought to be loans to borrowers at or below the median income in the area in which they lived. Fannie and Freddie became direct competition for the FHA, which insures low-and-moderate income (LMI) loans that are then securitized through Ginnie Mae. The affordable housing loans that Fannie and Freddie were required to buy were generally originated from the same group of LMI borrowers. Because of HUD's affordable-housing goals, by 2008 Fannie and Freddie held the credit risk—either through mortgages they retained in their portfolios or through mortgages they securitized and guaranteed—of 12 million subprime and Alt-A loans. These loans were about 40 percent of their single-family book of business. At the same time, the FHA had insured the credit risk for—and other government agencies held—about 5 million subprime and Alt-A loans.[6]

As a result of defaults on the subprime and other high-risk loans acquired under HUD's affordable-housing requirements, Fannie and Freddie are now insolvent. The U.S. Department of the Treasury has already contributed approximately $150 billion to cover their losses. Their regulator, the Federal Housing Finance Agency, has projected that Fannie and Freddie will eventually require between $221 and $363 billion in government support. This estimate may be optimistic and depends heavily on the direction of housing prices in the years ahead.

The Federal Housing Administration

BY THE LATE 1970s, the FHA's role had changed. Competition from the GSEs and private mortgage insurers had pushed the FHA out of the business of insuring middle-class mortgages; with the support of Congress, it began to concentrate increasingly on low-income borrowers and to see its role as an element of the government's social, rather than economic, policy. During the 1960s and 1970s, to meet its social responsibilities, it had significantly increased the LTV ratios of the mortgages it would insure and otherwise lowered its underwriting standards. Although these changes increased its credit risks, its losses were low because of the high rate of growth in housing values during this period. However, during the stagflation of the 1970s and the regional recessions of the 1980s, the FHA began to suffer substantial losses, requiring it to adopt tighter underwriting standards.

Still, as the government's authorized subprime lender, the FHA seems to believe it has an obligation to accept significant losses in pursuit of its mandate. Its claim rate has been high for many decades. Over a 35-year period (1975–2009), the agency's cumulative claim rate averaged 10.5 percent, and from 1992 to 2009 it averaged 10 percent. During the boom years of 1995–2003, the claim rate still averaged nearly 8 percent, while during bust periods (1980–85 and 2005–2008), it averaged 18 percent. For 2010–17, the FHA has projected an 8 percent average claim rate even with an expected 33 percent increase in home prices over 2011–20.[7] Although the FHA's accounting is difficult to penetrate and the agency claims its losses are fully covered by the fees it charges for insurance, a recent study by Barclays Capital suggests the imbedded losses at the FHA are substantial: "We project cumulative default rates in the 20 percent area on average, with loss given default rates of 60 percent. This represents average losses of about 12pts, of which 8.5pts could flow back to taxpayers. On an original balance of $1.4trn, this translates to $130bn."[8]

By the 1980s, the operations of both the FHA and the GSEs had created the beginnings of a national market—even an international market—in mortgages. Terms had been standardized, and the technology of securitization had been sufficiently developed such that it was possible for many kinds of institutional investors—insurance companies, pension funds, and mutual funds, as well as banks and other depositories—to hold conventional mortgages or MBS. In addition, Fannie and Freddie, perceived in the market as having the implicit backing of the U.S. government, provided an important bridge between mortgage originators and the ultimate investors by placing their guarantee on the securities backed by pools of mortgages (MBS). This guarantee eliminated the credit risk for these investors and facilitated the sale of the GSEs' MBS.

Also in the 1980s, while still following their charter requirements to invest only in loans "acceptable to institutional investors," Fannie and Freddie established underwriting standards for down payments, debt-to-income ratios, borrower information, and mortgage quality that limited their risks and kept delinquencies and defaults at low levels. However, the existence of the GSE guarantee created moral hazard that led to a lack of concern from both investors in the GSEs' MBS and the buyers of their debt securities about the quality of the loans they were buying. This allowed Fannie and Freddie—responding to the government requirements established by HUD—to acquire the vast numbers of subprime and Alt-A loans that caused their downfall.

Finally, in the Housing and Economic Recovery Act of 2008, which toughened the regulation of Fannie and Freddie, Congress increased the conforming loan limit for the GSEs in areas with high housing costs. The new limits in high-cost areas had the effect of increasing the size of the mortgages Fannie and Freddie could purchase so buyers of homes in the million-dollar range could have access to the benefits conferred by eligibility for purchase by the GSEs.

Summary

FROM THIS BRIEF survey, two facts stand out. First, the government role in housing finance has been successful in standardizing mortgage terms and creating a national market for mortgages, largely through the sale and distribution of MBS. This success has drawn financial resources from institutional investors in the United States and around the world, importantly supplementing the funds previously supplied primarily by banks and S&Ls. However, these benefits have come at a huge cost to U.S. taxpayers, who have been called upon in the past and will be called upon again to supply hundreds of billions of dollars to bail out the losses incurred by the government's financial support for housing.

DEFICIENCIES OF GOVERNMENT FINANCIAL SUPPORT FOR HOUSING

THESE MASSIVE GOVERNMENT losses occurred because government agencies have neither the incentives nor the means accurately to price the risks they are taking. Even if the government could price for risk like an insurance company, political pressures will not allow a government agency to accumulate during good times (as insurance companies do) the reserves necessary to meet its obligations during the inevitable bad times. This has been shown not only by the experience of the FHA but also by similar experiences at the Federal Deposit Insurance Corporation (FDIC),[9] the National Flood Insurance Program (NFIP),[10] and the Pension Benefit Guaranty Corporation (PBGC).[11] As a result, virtually every government intervention in the housing-finance market has resulted in substantial losses for taxpayers.

Many of the proposals on housing finance reform making the rounds in Washington today rely on government guarantees of MBS issued by special companies formed for the purpose of securitizing mortgages. These proposals are an obvious attempt to avoid the mistake of extending a government guarantee—implicit or explicit—to specific entities such as Fannie Mae and Freddie Mac. However, the Obama administration's plan, issued February 11, 2011, upset the expectation of many that it would adopt or develop a plan for the government's backing of MBS as a replacement for Fannie and Freddie.[12] Instead, the administration offered three options, one of which was a fully private-sector mortgage-financing system with a separate on-budget government program for assisting low-income homebuyers. Another option was the expected proposal for the government's backing of MBS issued by private-sector firms; the government's obligation would accrue only after the issuer's capital was wiped out. A third option was a private-sector system with a standby government backstop in case of a financial crisis.

Although it is difficult to assess the reasons for the administration's acceptance of the private-sector financing idea, the white paper issued by the administration suggested that it recognizes the danger to taxpayers implicit in any government guarantee program, including one that would guarantee only MBS. The danger is that a government guarantee will create moral hazard by eliminating investor concern about both the quality of the underlying loans and the financial capacity of the issuer; MBS buyers will not be concerned about either the quality of the underlying mortgages or the financial condition of the MBS issuers. To protect itself and taxpayers, the government would have to rely on regulation of the issuing firm, so that the issuer does not take excessive risk. As we have seen again and again, regulation has not worked to keep insured banks or the GSEs from taking risks, and there is no reason to believe it will prevent MBS issuers from doing the same. Accordingly, any continuing government support for housing finance is highly likely to result in massive taxpayer losses and, therefore, should be rejected as a sensible policy path.

Another reason for rejecting a government program to guarantee MBS, though not mentioned in the administration's white paper, is that government support for housing cannot be limited effectively. Government support is a subsidy from the taxpayers to the buyers and sellers of homes, no matter where in the process government support is injected, and as such, it confers a benefit on all homebuyers eligible to receive it. Accordingly, it is difficult—and probably impossible over the long term—to limit the availability of this benefit. No matter where the line is drawn, there will always be an excluded group. Inevitably, this produces political pressure to provide excluded groups with access to the benefits of the government support. Because these groups are always more organized than taxpayers as a whole, they eventually will be able to gain support in Congress for inclusion within the eligible category. In 1992, Congress adopted affordable-housing requirements for Fannie and Freddie so low-income and other borrowers who could not meet traditional mortgage standards would have access to the benefits the GSEs conferred on the middle class. Similarly, in the 2008 Housing and Economic Recovery Act, Congress conferred the same benefits on high-income constituents by increasing the conforming loan limits of the GSEs so they could buy mortgages on million-dollar homes in areas where housing prices were especially high.[13] Once a government subsidy program is established, it will expand to cover larger and larger portions of the population and simultaneously drive out competing private-sector activity, just as Fannie and Freddie drove private competition from the areas of the housing market in which they operated.

ARGUMENTS SUPPORTING GOVERNMENT INVOLVEMENT

JUDGING BY THE proposals circulating today in Washington, there is still a great deal of support for a continuing role for Fannie and Freddie or for a new system in which the government will still be responsible for backing some portion of the housing finance market. Given the deficiencies and taxpayer losses associated with past government efforts, what arguments are advanced to support another government financial support program for housing?

The easiest of these arguments to dismiss is also the one cited most—that government backing is necessary to ensure that a 30-year fixed-rate mortgage is available for homebuyers. This is simply a myth. Jumbo fixed-rate 30-year mortgages, which by definition are not government-backed, are freely available and advertised extensively on the Internet. A Google search for "jumbo 30 year fixed rate mortgage" turns up a host of offers. They may be somewhat more expensive than a government-backed 30-year fixed-rate mortgage, but that is only because taxpayers are subsidizing the government-backed version. Why it makes sense for taxpayers to subsidize mortgages people can freely get without taxpayer assistance is a puzzle, especially when that particular mortgage does not make much sense as a matter of public policy. It amortizes very slowly, so it does not create much equity in a home for many years (on average, Americans change residences every seven years), and at a time when we are finally recognizing the problems associated with excessive leverage in homeownership, the 30-year fixed-rate mortgage encourages maximum homeowner leverage.

Another argument for continued government involvement is that the mortgage market must be assured of a steady flow of funds or the process of building homes will be slowed or interrupted for periods when mortgage money is not readily available. But why does the housing business deserve to be protected against changes in the availability of funds when every other industry has to live with this cyclical problem? Moreover, the fact that housing finance has been protected all these years against the fluctuations every other industry has to bear probably has something to do with the bubbles to which this industry seems particularly prone. Concern about availability of funds would likely reduce overbuilding and speculation, and such a reduction is something government policy ought to encourage.

A third argument—explicit or implicit—is that institutional investors will buy U.S. mortgages or MBS only if they are supported by a government guarantee. This argument is probably the key reason for the support the government-guarantee idea enjoys in Washington, and it is true in regard to low-quality mortgages, and perhaps MBS backed by subprime or other low-quality mortgages. But as discussed later in this paper, there is no reason for mortgages allowed into the securitization system to be low quality. Until the introduction of the affordable-housing requirements for Fannie and Freddie, the GSEs maintained high underwriting standards and never suffered substantial losses on the mortgages they held or guaranteed. Even in the current crisis, their delinquency rates among prime mortgages have been under 3 percent, while their delinquency rates on subprime and Alt-A loans acquired because of the affordable-housing goals have ranged from 13.3 to 17.3 percent.[14] Accordingly, the key to a successful mortgage market is not a government guarantee—which will inevitably cause serious losses to taxpayers—but ensuring that new mortgages are of prime quality. Most important, it is clear from the Federal Reserve's Flow of Funds data that private institutional investors do not buy government-backed securities, including those issued by Fannie and Freddie, probably because their yields are too low.[15] The buyers tend to be foreign central banks, U.S. banks and S&Ls, and government pension plans, all of which are looking for safety rather than yield. Accordingly, the notion that investment in mortgages would increase if MBS were government-backed is incorrect. It is far more likely that a private mortgage market would produce mortgages with market yields that would be more attractive to private institutional investors—primarily insurance companies, pension funds, and mutual funds. These investors have $13 trillion dollars in fixed income investments, only seven percent of which is invested in GSE securities.[16]

Finally, the argument is made that we can provide the concessionary rates or other benefits that will enable low-income families to become homeowners only with government backing. This is true, but it does not mean the entire housing market has to be government backed—only the portion targeted to low-income homebuyers.

TABLE 1. THE PERFORMANCE OF EUROPEAN MORTGAGE MARKETS COMPARED WITH THE UNITED STATES

Country	Rate of Owner occupancy 2009 (%)	Coefficient of Covariation Housing Starts (%) [2]
Western Europe		
Austria	56.2	6.8
Belgium	78.0	15.9
Denmark	54.0	57.4
Finland	59.0	14.4
France	57.4	18.2
Germany	43.2	29.5
Ireland	74.5	84.2
Italy	80.0	25.7
Luxembourg	75.0	19.2
Netherlands	57.2	12.3
Norway	76.7	24.3
Portugal	76.0	27.2
Spain	85.0	60.5
Sweden	66.3	61.7
United Kingdom	69.5	13.9
European Average	**67.2**	**31.4**
United States	**67.2**	**40.0**
US rank	**8th of 16**	**5th of 16**

NOTES:

(1) Unless noted otherwise, the data are from European Mortgage Federation, Hypostat, 2009, http://hypo.org/Content/default.asp?PageID=524, a book that contains comprehensive mortgage and housing market data for the years 1998–2009 for 15 western European countries and the United States. (Statistical measures computed with annual data by country for the years 1998–2009).

(2) Computation based on housing starts where available; all other countries use housing permits.

(3) The mortgage interest rate for the European countries is each country's representative variable mortgage rate; see European Mortgage Federation, Hypostat. The U.S. rate is the Freddie Mac 1-year ARM commitment rate.

Standard Deviation of House-price Inflation (%)	Mortgage Interest Rate Average Level (%) [3]	Mortgage Interest Rate Average Spread (%) [4]	Outstanding Mortgage-to-GDP Ratio 2009 (%)
2.5	5.00	2.05	26.2
4.1	5.75	2.88	43.3
8.7	5.90	2.54	103.8
4.0	4.34	1.39	58.0
6.4	4.90	1.96	38.0
1.7	5.19	2.32	47.6
13.8	4.43	1.48	90.3
3.1	4.96	1.81	21.7
4.8	4.26	1.31	42.0
6.6	5.13	2.19	105.6
5.2	6.28	1.43	70.8
4.1	4.91	1.97	67.5
7.7	4.29	1.19	64.6
3.4	3.83	0.80	82.0
7.1	5.24	0.74	87.6
5.6	**4.96**	**1.74**	**63.3**
7.5	5.18	2.13	81.4
4th of 16	6th of 16	5th of 16	5th of 16

(4) The mortgage interest-rate spread equals the mortgage interest rate (column 4) relative to the Treasury bill rate of each country from the International Financial Statistics of the International Monetary Fund where available. Many of the euro area countries no longer publish independent Treasury bill rates; the French Treasury bill rate is used as the standard in these cases.

Source: European Mortgage federation, 2009; and International Financial Statistics, International Monetary Fund, 2009

WEIGHING THE POLICY ARGUMENTS FOR AND AGAINST GOVERNMENT BACKING

IF WE WEIGH taxpayer losses in the balance, the policy arguments in favor of government involvement in housing finance seem weak indeed. Over the nearly 70 years that the government has been attempting to assist housing finance, the taxpayers have been called upon to rescue one specially designed government program after another, and the costs—by the time the GSEs' and FHA's losses have been added up—run into the hundreds of billions of dollars. Yes, the United States did get a nationwide mortgage market, a standardized mortgage product, and an efficient system for turning a mortgage into a liquid investment, but the costs for the taxpayer have been horrific.

In other important areas, government involvement in the housing finance system has also been a failure. First, as shown in Table 1, prepared by Dwight M. Jaffee, the United States ranks 6th when compared with 15 Western European countries in terms of the average interest rate on residential mortgages. This result is remarkable, considering that the governments in most other developed countries provide no direct backing of mortgages. Moreover, government financial backing has not succeeded in raising the U.S. homeownership rate over the long term. This rate reached 64 percent in 1964 and remained there for 30 years. The rate began to climb when Fannie and Freddie were making subprime and Alt-A loans under the affordable-housing requirements imposed by Congress and administered by HUD, but since the insolvency of the GSEs (because of those very loans) and their inability to sustain affordable-housing lending, U.S. homeownership rates seem to be returning to the historic rate of 64 percent. Among Jaffee's list of countries, the United States ranks 8th of the 16 countries. In other words, U.S. taxpayers have received very little return for the huge costs they have borne.

Accordingly, there seems to be an overwhelming policy argument against continuing any government role in supporting housing finance. We have already realized all of the benefits we are likely to get from government involvement—a national mortgage market, standardized mortgages, and a workable system for bringing in funding from institutional investors—and it is likely that if we bring the government in again, we will face another taxpayer catastrophe in the future.

The only remaining questions are whether it will be possible to sustain a securitization system that allows institutional investors to support U.S. housing finance without a government guarantee on either mortgages or MBS and how a social policy of subsidizing homeownership for low-income families would fit into such a system.

A HOUSING FINANCE MARKET WITHOUT A GOVERNMENT ROLE

How would the housing market function without government support? The best way to start this analysis is to contrast the current state of the housing market with what prevailed in the past. We are now in the midst of the continuing deflation of a massive housing bubble, by far the largest housing bubble in our history. Figure 1 shows its growth between approximately 1997 and 2007, in comparison with past bubbles—all stated in terms of real (inflation-adjusted) dollars.

FIGURE 1. HOME-PRICE INDEX, 1890–2010

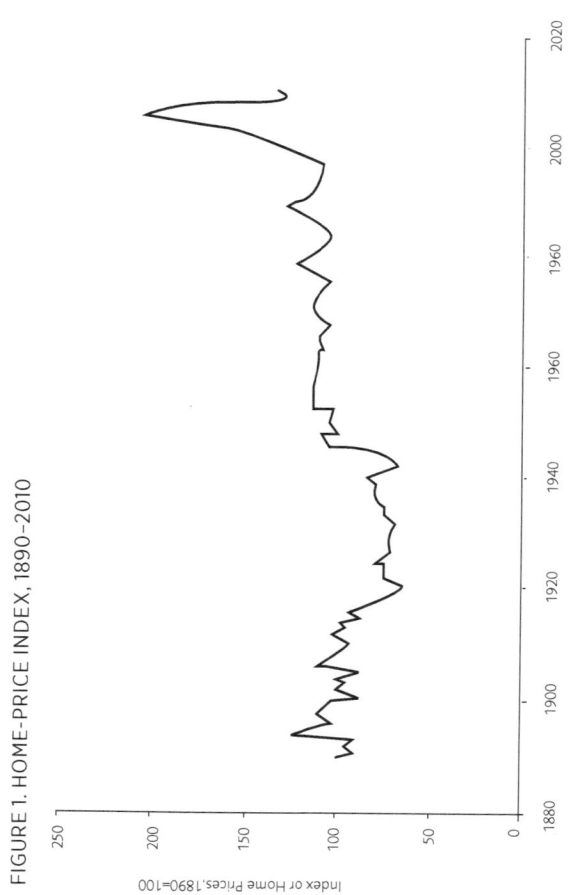

Source: Compiled from Robert Shiller's updated historical housing market data used in his book, Irrational Exuberance (Princeton University Press, 2000; Broadway Books, 2001; 2nd ed., 2005). Data available at http://www.econ.yale.edu/~shiller/data.htm.

Figure 1 shows at least three housing bubbles: one around 1980, another around 1990, and then the big one that started in about 1997, inflated until 2007, and is now quickly deflating. Why were the two earlier bubbles so small and short-lived compared to the most recent and destructive one?

As noted earlier, by 2008 the GSEs were exposed to the credit risk of 12 million subprime and Alt-A loans, while the FHA and other government agencies accounted for an additional 5 million. According to Edward Pinto's research, approximately 2.2 million loans of this kind were also made by banks under the Community Reinvestment Act (CRA) or by mortgage banks such as Countrywide under a HUD program that pledged them to use reduced down payments and underwriting standards generally in order to assist low-income families to buy homes. All these weak and high-risk loans are, in one way or another, the result of government policies.

An additional 7.8 million loans were securitized by Countrywide and others, sold through Wall Street underwriters, and were outstanding before the financial crisis. In an important sense, these loans were also the government's responsibility, because the funds the government poured into subprime and Alt-A loans during the 1990s and the first decade of 2000 drove the growth of the bubble, which in turn made it possible for Countrywide and others to originate and sell the private-label MBS that formed about one-third of the weak and high-risk mortgages outstanding. It is important to understand this mechanism. As bubbles grow, they tend to suppress delinquencies and defaults, because borrowers can always refinance or sell their homes for more than the mortgage

TABLE 2. OUTSTANDING SUBPRIME AND ALT-A LOANS, 2008

Entity	No. of Subprime and Alt-A Loans	Unpaid Principal Amount ($)
Fannie Mae and Freddie Mac	12 million	1.8 trillion
FHA and Other Federal*	5 million	0.6 trillion
CRA and HUD Programs	2.2 million	0.3 trillion
Total Federal Government	**19.2 million**	**2.7 trillion**
Other (Including Subprime and Alt-A Private MBS Issued by Countrywide, Wall Street, and Others)	7.8 million	1.9 trillion
Total	**27 million**	**4.6 trillion**

* *Includes Veterans Administration, Federal Home Loan Banks, and other federal programs.*

Source: Edward Pinto, "Sizing Total Federal Government and Federal Agency Contributions to Subprime and Alt-A Loans in U.S. First Mortgage Market as of 6.30.08: Exhibit 2 with Corrections through 10.11.10" 4, http://www.aei.org/docLib/PintoFCICTriggersMemo.pdf.

amount when housing prices are rising. Accordingly, by the early 2000s investors noticed that while subprime and other low-quality mortgages were producing high yields because of their supposed risks, they were not showing commensurate defaults. In other words, MBS backed by subprime and other weak mortgages looked like good investments. This situation stimulated the growth of a market in MBS backed by these low-quality mortgages—the first time such a market had ever developed. When the bubble began to deflate, the mortgages in these private MBS began to default in unprecedented numbers, causing the weakness in financial institutions that we know as the financial crisis.[17]

Thus, as a direct or indirect consequence of government policies, approximately 27 million subprime and Alt-A loans were outstanding in the United States before the financial crisis—about half of all U.S. mortgages. Table 2 summarizes these numbers and the dollar amounts involved.

The composition of the earlier bubbles differed dramatically. The 1980 bubble occurred at a time when subprime mortgages were very rare and Alt-A mortgages were almost nonexistent. When that bubble collapsed, foreclosure starts, according to Mortgage Bankers Association data, peaked at 0.87 percent in 1983.[18] When the 1990 bubble collapsed, subprime and other high-risk loans were still rare and foreclosure starts peaked at 1.32 percent in 1994.[19] However, in the case of the 1997–2007 bubble, almost half of which consisted of subprime or otherwise weak and high-risk loans, foreclosure starts reached 5.3 percent in 2009 even though the government had established a number of programs to prevent or reduce foreclosures.

In other words, there is very strong evidence that ensuring that mortgages are of prime quality greatly reduces the likelihood of a large and long-lived bubble. Indeed, the delinquency rates on the GSEs' prime loans averaged 2.6 percent for Fannie and 2.0 percent for Freddie in 2009, while the delinquency rates on their nonprime loans averaged 17.3 and 13.8 percent, respectively.[20] These delinquency rates lead to the conclusion that one way to ensure that a securitization system for housing finance will work—without government financial backing—is simply to ensure that the vast preponderance of mortgages, and all securitized mortgages, are of prime quality. Prime-quality mortgages are good investments. Historically, and even during the financial crisis, prime mortgages did not suffer high rates of delinquency. For this reason, after the markets return to normal, there should be no difficulty in placing MBS based on prime-quality mortgages with institutional investors in the United States and around the world.

Regulation is necessary in this case because there is strong evidence of market failure in the history of housing bubbles. As noted above, bubbles tend to suppress defaults and encourage lenders and borrowers to believe, "This time is different." Borrowers seek to keep their down payments and monthly payments low over the short term with riskier loans while trying to buy homes that have become more expensive. Lenders believe the increasing value of homes limits their risk even on riskier mortgages. Investors—who do not see any increase in delinquencies while the bubble is growing (because higher home prices allow homeowners who cannot meet their mortgage obligations to sell or refinance their houses)—are willing to buy MBS backed by subprime loans. As we have seen, all these market participants are wrong. Inside the bubble, risks are growing substantially, and when the bubble finally deflates the losses can be so severe that, as we saw in 2008, serious financial panic erupts. Appropriate regulation can break this cycle by requiring that all securitized mortgages meet certain quality tests.

The necessary regulation would not be complicated. It would require all securitized mortgages to be of prime quality. That means the borrower, among other requirements, (1) will make a 10–20 percent down payment or, for a refinance, will have equity in the home of at least 20 percent, (2) has a debt-to-income ratio of no more than 38 percent, and (3) has a credit score of at least 660. It should be noted, too, that an otherwise prime loan may be weakened substantially by a second mortgage. In effect, a second lien increases the LTV ratio of the first lien. This problem could be addressed by requiring that second mortgages not be added to a property without the approval of the first lien holder.

The rules would be less stringent for loans held in the portfolios of banks and other financial institutions, but the quality of mortgages outstanding should be disclosed so market participants are aware of how many do not meet prime standards. This disclosure would allow them to estimate the severity of any subsequent downturn.[21]

EXAMPLES FROM ABROAD

REGULATION OF THIS kind is what makes other housing finance systems work as well as they do. The United States is one of very few developed countries to back residential mortgages in any way, and the others that do supply some backing tend to provide liquidity support rather than credit support. Most developed countries, in Europe and elsewhere, rely on regulations that control mortgage quality to ensure that their mortgage systems work.[22] Denmark provides a case in point. It has an interesting system in which mortgage banks arrange for mortgages and take the credit risk, but the mortgages are funded in the open market as part of a pool of mortgages of the same tenor. The quality of the mortgages that go into the system is strictly controlled, and because the mortgage banks assume the credit risk, their interests are aligned with those of the buyers of the MBS issued by the mortgage pool. Germany has a covered-bond system that also rests on regulations that strictly control the quality of the mortgages allowed entrance. Neither the Danish nor German government backs any part of the mortgage financing system, but both systems seem to work well because of the regulatory assurances of mortgage quality. In over 200 years, not one mortgage bank has failed in Denmark, nor has Germany suffered a failure to meet covered-bond obligations.

LENDING TO LOW-INCOME BORROWERS

How would a social policy that provided government assistance for low-income families fare in this environment? First, note that there is no internal inconsistency between a system that relies primarily on high-quality mortgages for steady functioning and a social policy that encourages making concessionary loans to low-income borrowers. Unless Congress creates a new system, the FHA could continue to function as the insurer for loans to low-income borrowers. But certain restrictions would be necessary to protect taxpayers, borrowers, and firms that operate in the prime market.

First, all FHA commitments should be on budget so Congress and taxpayers have an idea of the liabilities the FHA is assuming. The FHA's obligations are currently covered by the Federal Credit Reform Act, but its accounting is very complex, making it difficult to determine something as simple as whether its assets exceed its liabilities. Second, while the quality standards for FHA mortgages would be lower than those in the prime market, the agency cannot be allowed to function without quality standards. Taxpayers should take some risks in support of social policies deemed worthwhile for the country as a whole, but Congress has a responsibility to limit the size of these risks. In other words, lower credit scores would be expected, but there would have to be a minimum. Down payments could be lower than for prime mortgages. Finally, the FHA should not compete with private originators or securitizers. They should be seen as functioning in two different markets. For example, the FHA's support might be limited to borrowers at or below 80 percent of the median income in the area in which they live and loan sizes might be restricted to 100 percent of the median home price.

ELIMINATING FANNIE AND FREDDIE

FINALLY, IF WE were to adopt a housing finance system that relies on mortgage quality rather than a government guarantee to foster the sale of MBS, would Fannie and Freddie have any role? The answer is no. By helping to standardize mortgages and by creating a national and international market for U.S. residential mortgages, Fannie and Freddie have fulfilled their mandate. A secondary market for jumbo mortgages exists and there is no reason that market cannot be extended into the conforming market now dominated by the GSEs.

One of the advantages of a comprehensive reform of the housing finance market along the lines described in this paper is that it significantly simplifies the process of eliminating or privatizing Fannie and Freddie. Regulating the quality of mortgages so that we overcome the tendency of a housing market to create bubbles—and especially the tendency of a government-backed market to create large and potentially dangerous bubbles—will make it possible to eliminate the GSEs simply by reducing their conforming loan limits gradually over time. As the GSEs are gradually withdrawn from the housing finance market, private securitization of prime mortgages will take their place. The AEI white paper mentioned earlier recommends a reduction of 20 percent per year in both the regular and the high-cost GSE conforming loan limits.

Of course, at this point, the securitization market is extremely weak; few deals are going forward. Many commentators note that without a robust securitization market, the plan for reforming the housing market along the lines outlined in this paper would not be workable. I agree, but, theoretically, there is no reason the securitization of mortgages should not return to health once the quality of mortgages is reestablished. MBS backed by these mortgages are likely to be sought-after investments for institutional investors. Indeed, a January 15, 2011, article in the *New York Times* noted that the spread between the GSE rate for a 30-year fixed-rate mortgage and the nongovernment rate for a jumbo fixed-rate mortgage was only 60 basis points and coming down.[23] This information is significant. It suggests that the securitization market is beginning to revive. A 60 basis-point spread is high, but it has come down considerably from where it was after the financial crisis. Additionally, the GSE rate may be artificially low because of the current government subsidization of the GSEs. In connection with the preparation of the AEI white paper, my coauthors and I consulted extensively with institutional investors, securitizers, and mortgage insurers. We found that institutional investors were eager to invest in mortgages that yielded a market rate, and securitizers would price a prime mortgage—backed by mortgage insurance—at 25–40 basis points higher than the equivalent Fannie Mae mortgage. We believe this rate will attract institutional investors.

Assuming that a robust securitization market develops, the following steps would provide a workable way to wind down the GSEs:

- The law would provide for a reduction in the GSEs' conforming loan limit by 20 percent of the previous year's cap each year, starting with the current general limit for one-unit properties of $417,000 and the high-cost area limit of $729,750. If we assume an 80-percent LTV ratio, the current limits allow mean house prices of over $500,000 and $900,000, respectively. In contrast, according to the National Association of Realtors, the median U.S. house price is $170,600.[24]

- Under this conforming-loans reductions schedule, the general limit for a one-unit property would decrease to $334,000 in year one, $267,000 in year two, $214,000 in year three, $171,200 in year four, and finally to $136,960 in year five. The high-cost area limit for a one-unit property would decrease to $584,000 in year one, $467,000 in year two, $374,000 in year three, $299,200 in year four, and to $240,800 in year five.

- As the GSEs withdraw from markets larger than the conforming loan limits, private securitization will assume the role of providing a secondary market. If only prime mortgages are involved in these securitizations, the MBS should be attractive investments for banks, insurance companies, pension funds, mutual funds, and other institutional investors.

- Final termination, or "sunset," of GSE status would take place at the end of year five.

- From the beginning of their winding down, the GSEs would be prohibited from adding to their portfolios of mortgages or MBS. These would be allowed to run off naturally, although if the market is strong enough, the GSEs could sell them. The GSEs would not be permitted to hold loans or MBS in the GSEs' portfolios, except for short periods as necessary to support MBS issuance.

- During the winding-down period, Fannie and Freddie would be allowed to buy only prime loans and, to prevent them from arbitraging their GSE status, they would be permitted to invest only in short-term Treasury bills.

- At the sunset date, a liquidating trust would be created containing all remaining mortgage assets, guaranty liabilities, and debt. The trust would hold Treasury securities to be liquidated if necessary to meet the trust's obligations. When the last mortgage is refinanced or sold by the trustee, the trust will be terminated and any remaining Treasury securities will be returned to the Treasury. Taxpayers will unjustly—but at this point unavoidably—bear the GSE net-worth shortfall, including the Treasury's writing off of its preferred stock.

- All of Fannie and Freddie's intellectual property, systems, securitization platforms, goodwill, customer relationships, and organizational capital should be auctioned off in a termination or privatization. The proceeds would reduce the Treasury's and taxpayers' losses.

CONCLUSION

THE HISTORY OF government support for housing finance shows that it invariably results in massive taxpayer losses while producing very few of the benefits for the country—such as increases in homeownership or lower interest rates for housing finance—that the government seeks. Instead of basing the financing of housing on government backing, a robust system of housing finance can be based on ensuring the quality of mortgages. Other developed countries generally structure their residential housing finance systems this way, and in so doing they achieve better outcomes than the United States does without any substantial taxpayer costs. The administration's acceptance of this idea—at least as an option—is a major advance in that it enables those in Congress who are unwilling to support another government-backed system to make common cause with the administration. Once this system is adopted and rules are in place to ensure mortgage quality, Fannie and Freddie can be gradually withdrawn from the market by reducing the conforming loan limit over a period of five years. As that happens, it is highly likely that the private sector will take over the areas from which the GSEs have withdrawn.

NOTES

1. Kerry D. Vandell, "FHA Restructuring Proposals: Alternatives and Implications," *Fannie Mae Housing Policy Debate* 6, no. 2 (1995).
2. Ibid.
3. *Depository Institutions Deregulation and Monetary Control Act of 1980*, Public Law 96-221, 96th Cong., 2d sess. (March 31, 1980).
4. Section 1719 of Fannie's charter states: "The operations of the corporation . . . shall be confined . . . to mortgages which are deemed by the corporation to be of such quality, type, and class as to meet, generally, the *purchase standards imposed by private institutional mortgage investors*" [emphasis added]. See *Fannie Mae Charter Act*, codified at U.S. Code 12 (1938) §1719, http://www.fanniemae.com/aboutfm/pdf/charter.pdf.
5. *Housing and Community Development Act of 1992*, Public Law 102-550, 102nd Cong., 2d sess. (October 28, 1992).
6. Edward Pinto, "Sizing Total Federal Government and Federal Agency Contributions to Subprime and Alt-A Loans in U.S. First Mortgage Market as of 6.30.08," http://www.aei.org/docLib/PintoFCICTriggersMemo.pdf.
7. U.S. Department of Housing and Urban Development, *FHA Actuarial Review of the Mutual Mortgage Insurance Fund*, FY 2010 and FY 2000 reviews, http://portal.hud.gov/hudportal/HUD?src=/program_offices/housing/rmra/oe/rpts/actr/actrmenu.
8. Barclays, "U.S. Housing Finance: No Silver Bullet," December 13, 2010, 6.
9. When the deposit insurance system was reformed in 1991 in response to the failure of the Federal Savings and Loan Insurance Corporation, Congress limited the size of the deposit insurance fund the FDIC could accumulate to meet the demands of a future crisis. Since 1996, the FDIC has been prohibited by law from charging premiums to well-capitalized and stable institutions. As a result, between 1996 and 2006, institutions representing 98 percent

of deposits paid no deposit insurance premiums. When the financial crisis hit in 2008, the FDIC's insurance fund was inadequate to meet the losses incurred. Instead, once the bad times hit, the FDIC was forced to raise its premiums at the worst possible moment, thereby reinforcing the impact of the down cycle. See Center on Federal Financial Institutions (COFFI), "Federal Deposit Insurance Corporation" (Washington, DC: COFFI, August 10, 2005), http://www.coffi.org/pubs/Summaries/FDIC%20Summary.pdf. See also Congressional Budget Office, "Modifying Federal Deposit Insurance," May 9, 2005, http://www.cbo.gov/doc.cfm?index=6342&type=0, which says, "Currently, 93 percent of FDIC-insured institutions, which hold 98 percent of insured deposits, pay nothing for deposit insurance."

10. Thomas Fink, "Huge Losses Put Federal Flood Insurance Plan in the Red," *USA Today*, August 26, 2010. "FEMA Administrator Craig Fugate says the debt results partly from Congress restraining insurance rates to encourage the purchase of coverage, which is required for property owners with a federally backed mortgage. . . . 'It is not run as a business,' Fugate said. Congress' Government Accountability Office said in April that the program is 'by design, not actuarially sound' because it has no cash reserves to pay for catastrophes such as Katrina and sets rates that 'do not reflect actual flood risk.' Raising insurance rates or limiting coverage is hard. 'The board of directors of this program is Congress,' Fugate said. 'They are very responsive to individuals who are being adversely affected.'"

11. At the end of FY 2010, the PBGC reported a deficit of $23 billion in its 2010 annual report, saying, "In part, it is a result of the fact that the premiums PBGC charges are insufficient to pay for all the benefits that PBGC insures, and other factors." See Pension Benefit Guaranty Corporation, *2010 PBGC Annual Report* (Washington, DC: PBGC, November 12, 2010), http://www.pbgc.gov/documents/ar2010.htm.

12. U.S. Departments of Treasury and Housing and Community Development, *Reforming America's Housing Finance Market: A Report to Congress* (Washington, DC: Treasury and HCD, February 2011), http://www.treasury.gov/initiatives/Documents/Reforming%20America%27s%20Housing%20Finance%20Market.pdf.

13. *Housing and Economic Recovery Act of 2008*, Public Law 110–289, 110th Cong., 2d sess. (July 30, 2008).

14. Edward J. Pinto, "Government Housing Policies in the Lead-up to the Financial Crisis: A Forensic Study" (discussion draft, American Enterprise Institute, Washington, DC, November 4, 2010), chart 53, http://www.aei.org/docLib/Government-Housing-Policies-Financial-Crisis-Pinto-102110.pdf.

15. U.S. Federal Reserve, *Flow of Funds Accounts of the United States*, March 10, 2011, 90, table L.210, "Agency- and GSE-Backed Securities (1),"

http://www.federalreserve.gov/releases/z1/20110310/z1r-4.pdf.

16. Peter J. Wallison, "Government Mortgage Guarantees Are Unnecessary," *Wall Street Journal*, April 21, 2011.

17. For a complete discussion of this process, see Peter J. Wallison, *Dissent from the Majority Report of the Financial Crisis Inquiry Commission* (Washington, DC: American Enterprise Institute, January 26, 2011), http://www.aei.org/paper/100190.

18. Mortgage Bankers Association (MBA), *National Delinquency Survey* (Washington, DC: MBA, 1983).

19. MBA, *National Delinquency Survey*, (Washington, DC: MBA, 1994).

20. Pinto, "Government Housing Policies in the Lead-up to the Financial Crisis," chart 53.

21. For a complete discussion of reforming the housing finance market along these lines, see Peter J. Wallison, Alex J. Pollock, and Edward J. Pinto, "Taking the Government out of Housing Finance: Principles for Reforming the Housing Finance Market" (white paper, American Enterprise Institute, Washington, DC, March 24, 2011), http://www.aei.org/paper/100206.

22. Barclays Capital U.S. Securitized Products, "U.S. Housing Finance: No Silver Bullet," Outlook 2011, figure 3.

23. Jennifer Saranow Schultz, "BUCKS; The Jumbo Rate Gap Shrinks," *New York Times*, January 15, 2011, http://query.nytimes.com/gst/fullpage.html?res=9500E4DE153CF936A25752C0A9679D8B63.

24. National Association of Realtors, *Median Sales Price of Existing Single-Family Homes for Metropolitan Areas*, 4th quarter 2010, http://www.realtor.org/wps/wcm/connect/5e37be0045ba291385f5c7342c47dc89/REL10Q4T_rev.pdf?MOD=AJPERES&CACHEID=5e37be0045ba291385f5c7342c47dc89.

THE WAY FORWARD: U.S. RESIDENTIAL-MORTGAGE FINANCE IN A POST-GSE WORLD

LAWRENCE J. WHITE*

THE INSOLVENCIES AND conservatorships of Fannie Mae and Freddie Mac in September 2008 clearly established the inappropriateness of the government-sponsored enterprise (GSE) model for residential-mortgage finance in the United States. Three years later, however, the $5 trillion question—how to replace their presence in the secondary mortgage market—remains unanswered.[1]

This chapter will lay out a vision for how private markets would—if given the opportunity—replace the GSEs and provide a fully functioning secondary market for residential mortgages.[2] In the event that the private sector is deemed inadequate for the task, this paper also proposes a side-by-side private-plus-government form of mortgage guarantee that would be superior to the "tail risk" or

---

* Thanks are due to Kim Schoenholtz and three anonymous reviewers for useful comments on an earlier draft and to John Pulito for research assistance. During 1986–89, I served as a board member on the Federal Home Loan Bank Board and, in that capacity, also served as a board member of Freddie Mac.

"catastrophic" government insurance proposals that have circulated as alternatives to the GSEs.[3]

THE BASICS OF RESIDENTIAL MORTGAGE FINANCE[4]

A BRIEF REVIEW of the basics of residential mortgage finance should prove useful for the discussion that follows.

Credit Risk

THE FUNDAMENTAL QUESTION for lenders in any lending arrangement is, "Will I get my money back?" This question is usually described as involving "credit risk." A number of observable factors influence the degree of credit risk in a mortgage-lending arrangement:

- The collateral. The house serves as collateral for the loan, which decreases the credit risk for the lender.[5] But the house may lose value after the loan has been made, which would increase credit risk for the lender.

- The proportion of the house's value that is funded by the mortgage, which is known as the loan-to-value (LTV) ratio. At the beginning of the mortgage arrangement, LTV can be measured as the reciprocal of the percentage down payment that the buyer makes on the house. Thus, the larger the down payment percentage is, the lower the LTV. The larger down payment (lower LTV) provides a larger initial buffer that better protects the lender against a subsequent fall in the house's value and thereby reduces the credit risk for the lender.[6] The subsequent LTV (and buffer for the lender) will depend on the borrower's pattern of paying down the principal and changes in the value of the house. Since a lower LTV also means that the borrower has a greater equity stake in the house, the borrower is less likely to default on paying the mortgage.[7]

- The mortgage's length (term). The longer the term is, the slower the pay-down of the loan principal, and the higher the probability that the borrower might default with negative equity.[8]

- The borrower's prospective income.

- The percentage of the borrower's monthly income that is required to make the monthly mortgage payment.

- The borrower's other debt obligations.[9]

- The borrower's other assets.[10]

- The borrower's credit history.

- The borrower's employment history.

Unobservable factors are also likely to influence the degree of credit risk in a mortgage-lending arrangement. There is an information asymmetry between the borrower and the lender in that the borrower knows more about her repayment likelihood than the lender does.[11] Thus, before making the loan, the lender faces an adverse selection problem in trying to determine who is most likely to repay the loan; after making the loan, the lender may have difficulty in monitoring the borrower to see if her ability to repay the loan has changed, which is a moral-hazard problem. A repayment schedule that requires monthly payments (as opposed to, for example, a single balloon payment at the end of the loan term) provides some reassurance to the lender; equivalently, a borrower's failure to make a monthly payment may be an early-warning signal that something has changed with respect to her repayment ability.

Interest-Rate Risk

SINCE A MORTGAGE is typically a long-term lending arrangement, it involves interest-rate risk. As market interest rates for similar debt instruments change during the loan's term, one side of the mortgage transaction will be worse off and the other side will be better off. For example, if market interest rates increase during the term of a fixed-rate mortgage (FRM), the lender is worse off (the lender is earning less than the current opportunity costs), while the borrower is better off (the borrower is paying less than the current opportunity costs). For an FRM, the level of interest-rate risk increases with the term of the loan.

With an adjustable-rate mortgage (ARM), the borrower's interest rate changes in accordance with an index that is linked to market interest rates, so the borrower bears the entire interest-rate risk.[12] With an FRM (and if the borrower is not allowed to prepay the mortgage), the interest-rate risk is shared between the lender and the borrower: as noted, if interest rates go up, the borrower gains and the lender loses. In contrast, if interest rates fall below the contract rate for an FRM, the lender benefits (since the FRM is now a more valuable asset), but the borrower loses (since the borrower is paying interest at a rate that is now above current market rates).

However, in the United States, a mortgage borrower always has the opportunity—the option—to prepay all or part of her mortgage. Effectively, this is a call option that the borrower pays for, either at the time of loan origination in the form of a higher interest rate or at the time of prepayment in the form of a fee.[13] If a borrower has complete flexibility of prepayment, then with an FRM all of the interest-rate risk is borne by the lender.[14] In addition to having a less valuable asset when interest rates rise above the contract rate, the lender does not get the benefit when interest rates decline below the contract rate since the borrower will be more likely to pay off the mortgage and refinance at the lower rate. However, if the borrower must pay a fee at the time of prepayment, the borrower is less likely to prepay (and the lender receives an explicit payment in the event that the borrower does prepay), and the lender's interest-rate risk is reduced.

Addressing Credit Risk

DIFFERENT STRUCTURES FOR mortgage lending address credit risk in different ways.

The Traditional Lending Structure

PRIOR TO THE 1980s, the predominant form of mortgage lending in the United States involved a depository institution—a savings institution or a commercial bank—that originated the mortgage loan and held the loan in its own portfolio, financing the loan through the gathering of deposits. The depository institution dealt directly with the borrower and developed expertise in deciding who was a creditworthy borrower and who was not. In essence, this was a vertically integrated lending process: the origination and investment decisions all occurred within the same organization. Thus, the organization that originated the loan would also bear the costs of poor lending decisions and thereby had a direct incentive to try to make good decisions.

The Newer Securitization Structure

WITH SECURITIZATION, THE lending process has become vertically disintegrated: the mortgage originator does not hold the loan in portfolio but instead sells it to a securitizer.[15] The securitizer buys multiple mortgages and bundles (or pools) them into a multi-mortgage security, which is sold to investors. The investors have a claim on the stream of interest and principal repayments from the underlying mortgages (which are the collateral for the securities),[16] and the investors are the ultimate source of financing—the effective lenders—for the mortgage borrowers.[17] But the investors are usually not specialists in the skills of origination (mortgage lending) and, in any event, are separated from the borrowers by at least two levels: the originators and the securitizer. Accordingly, the basic issue of credit risk arises: how can the investors in mortgage-backed securities (MBS) be reassured of getting their money back?

One strategy is that rather than buying individual mortgages—which might involve a great deal of idiosyncratic risk[18]—the investors are buying claims on multiple (usually hundreds of) mortgages; consequently, the law of large numbers is likely to provide the benefit of diversification and reduce greatly the idiosyncratic risk element. Also, a package of mortgages can provide geographic diversification to dampen the consequences of local economic shocks.[19]

Also, the originators may offer detailed information ("representations and warranties") about the quality of the underlying mortgages that have gone into the MBS. But the investors may not be familiar with the originators or their reputations, and the possibility of an originator's bankruptcy would limit the value of any prior assurances. Consequently, the investors are more likely to look to the securitizer from whom they directly purchase for reassurance. So, how can the securitizer reassure the investors as to credit risk?

One simple solution is for the government to provide an explicit guarantee to the investors. This has been the route undertaken by the Government National Mortgage Association (Ginnie Mae), which is an agency within the U.S. Department of Housing and Urban Development (HUD) that guarantees MBS that are based on mortgage loans that have been insured by the Federal Housing Administration (FHA) or the U.S. Department of Veterans Affairs (VA).[20] In essence, this guarantee pushes the credit risk onto the government guarantor. However, if the government guarantor mismanages the credit risk, it becomes a problem for taxpayers.

A quite similar solution was to have GSEs Fannie Mae and Freddie Mac be the securitizers and directly provide the guarantees.[21] Though the two companies were organized as "normal" corporations, with tens of thousands of shareholders and stock that was traded on the New York Stock Exchange, these companies had enough special features that the financial markets treated them (including the guarantees on the MBS that they issued) as carrying an implicit guarantee from the federal government—which reassured the investors, allowing the GSEs to pay lower interest rates on their obligations.[22] In the end, this belief turned out to be correct, and the credit-risk problem that the GSEs took over from the MBS investors has indeed become the taxpayers' problem.[23]

In the absence of government guarantees (explicit or implicit), private-label securitizers have had to devise alternative methods for reassuring investors. The most prominent method has been to partition, or tranche, the securities. Tranching creates a junior security that is the first to absorb losses from defaults by the underlying mortgage borrowers and a senior security that is buffered by the junior security against those initial default losses (until the losses have mounted so high as to absorb all of the investment in the junior security).[24] In essence, the junior security provides protection for the senior security, and the relative size of the junior security is crucial for determining the extent of the protection for—the riskiness of—the senior security (for any given quality of the underlying collateral).[25]

Additional methods of providing reassurance to MBS investors include guarantees from financially strong third parties (such as insurance companies) for some or all of the tranches of a security; the overcollateralization of the mortgage pool, so as to provide an additional equity buffer to protect the MBS holders; and the "excess spread"—the difference between what the mortgage borrowers pay in interest and what the MBS investors receive—that can be placed in a reserve account to provide a buffer for investors. These methods are not mutually exclusive (nor are they incompatible with tranching).

Further, unless they have sufficient analytical skills of their own, nonspecialist MBS investors are likely to seek independent third-party advice as to the creditworthiness of the securities (or the appropriateness of the tranching structure, given the quality of the underlying collateral and other factors) from credit rating agencies or other creditworthiness advisory services.[26]

Addressing Interest-Rate Risk

AS DISCUSSED EARLIER, with FRMs, the lender—either the depository institution in the traditional model or the securities investor in the securitization model—bears some or all of the interest-rate risk. Since the typical FRM has a 30-year term, this risk is substantial. Indeed, it was insufficient attention to these risks on the part of savings institutions and policy makers that initially caused the savings and loan (S&L) industry's woes in the late 1970s and early 1980s.[27] Since that time, depository institutions have been encouraged by their prudential regulators to try to hedge their interest-rate risk (for example, through the use of interest-rate derivatives), to originate and hold more ARMs, or to sell their FRMs into the secondary market.

Under the securitization model, the securities holders bear the interest-rate risk. In turn, the investors can hedge these risks with interest-rate derivatives. Alternatively, the cash flows from the underlying mortgages can be sliced and diced so that some investors are more buffered from interest-rate risk while other investors are more exposed.[28]

As discussed, the borrower'soption to prepay all or part of the mortgage places additional interest-rate risk onto the lender (or onto the MBS investor in the securitization model). In essence, the ability to prepay is an option that either is paid for explicitly through a prepayment fee at the time the option is exercised (that is, at the time of prepayment) or is paid for at the time of origination through a higher interest rate (which would likely reflect the lender's expectation of the costs of the borrower's exercising the option). A system of explicit prepayment fees thus reduces the lender's interest-rate risk and translates into lower interest rates for borrowers.[29]

THE WAY FORWARD

IN ORDER TO consider alternatives to the GSE system, it is worthwhile to begin with a statement of the appropriate goals for a housing finance system—including a statement of what ought *not* to be the goals of housing finance.

The Appropriate Goals of a Housing Finance System

FUNDAMENTALLY, HOUSING FINANCE should embody the

true societal costs—the opportunity costs—of lending for home purchases. Those costs encompass the fundamental time value of money, the costs of credit risk (that is, the probabilities and costs of nonrepayment), the costs of interest-rate risks, and the costs associated with a mortgage's being a relatively illiquid instrument.

Equally important is what a housing finance system should not try to do:

- It should not try to address the positive social externalities or spillover effects from homeownership (such as homeowners' greater likelihood of becoming involved in community governance issues). Those externalities are better addressed by separate programs that address the externalities more directly—for example, programs that specifically encourage otherwise qualified low- and moderate-income households to become first-time homeowners.[30]

- It should not try to be a vehicle for income redistribution. Income redistribution is best addressed through explicit programs that involve cash transfers rather than in-kind transfers and subsidies. Thus, an emphasis on affordable housing should not be part of the housing finance system.

- It should not try to be a vehicle for maintaining residential property values.

- It should not try to be a vehicle for supporting

employment in the home-building, real-estate, or mortgage-lending industries. [31]

Buffering the U.S. Economy from a Housing Collapse

THE DEFLATION AND then collapse of the U.S. housing bubble, beginning in 2006, has had devastating consequences for the U.S. economy. Although it would seem that the avoidance of a similar collapse in the future ought also to be a goal of a housing finance system, that goal may be too difficult. However, buffering the U.S. economy from the consequences of a collapse—or at least greatly reducing the consequences—is a reasonable goal. But that goal should be achieved outside of housing finance, through better prudential regulation—especially higher capital requirements—for large, systemic financial institutions.

Compare the consequences of two recent market collapses: the collapse of technology stocks in the late 1990s and the recent collapse in housing prices. Both collapses were of surprisingly equal magnitudes: their aggregate losses were about $7 trillion each.[32] However, their consequences were nowhere near comparable. The former collapse led to a comparatively mild recession of the U.S. economy; the latter collapse led to the Great Recession, the reverberations of which are still being felt strongly, especially with respect to U.S. unemployment.

Why the difference? The losses from the bursting of the tech bubble were largely absorbed by households through the equities that they held directly, in mutual funds and pension funds. In essence these were unleveraged holdings. The losses were borne; the households were poorer; they lowered their spending; there were negative, but comparatively mild, macroeconomic consequences; and the economy moved on.

In contrast, although most housing-collapse losses have been absorbed by households during the Great Recession, a nontrivial fraction of the losses—about $1.3 trillion—have been transferred to the financial sector through mortgage defaults and the consequent losses on the mortgages and MBS that have experienced defaults.[33] This $1.3 trillion in losses has devastated the financial sector, because it contains important parts (specifically, depository institutions, investment banks, the GSEs, and [to a more limited extent] insurance companies) that are thinly capitalized (highly leveraged) and that did not have sufficient capital (in essence, net worth) to absorb the losses. Those losses and the fears of consequent insolvencies and bankruptcies, compounded by uncertainties over whom, exactly, would bear the losses, caused the financial sector to freeze in the late summer of 2008. In turn, the U.S. stock market collapsed (which greatly magnified the loss of wealth for U.S. households), inflicting far greater damage on the U.S. economy.

There is, then, an important lesson from this comparison of the two bubbles' collapses: regardless of the housing finance system that replaces the GSEs, financial sector regulation must be greatly strengthened—with higher capital levels—so that the sector can survive even a collapse of great magnitude.

A Largely Private Residential-Mortgage Finance System[34]

A LARGELY PRIVATE residential-mortgage finance system

would have two major components: financing through depository institutions and financing through private securitizations.[35]

Financing through Depository Institutions

WHAT IS OFTEN forgotten in the discussion of the future of mortgage finance is that the traditional vertically integrated form of mortgage finance through depository institutions remains a significant part of the U.S. mortgage system. As of year-end 2007 (before the financial crisis), U.S. depository institutions held 30 percent of the value of all outstanding single-family mortgages.[36] This share was surely adversely affected by the special advantages that the GSEs had vis-à-vis the depository institutions: the GSEs could borrow at especially favorable rates because of their GSE status; they had lower capital requirements (2.5 percent) for holding whole mortgages in their portfolios than did the depository institutions (4 percent); and the GSEs were required to hold only 0.45 percent capital against the credit risk on their MBS on which they issued guarantees (and if the depository institutions chose to hold the GSEs' MBS in their portfolios instead of whole loans, they were required to hold only 1.6 percent capital instead of 4 percent).[37]

Without the GSEs and their special advantages, the depositories' share of the residential-mortgage market would likely be at least as large as their 30 percent share in 2007 and probably larger. The depositories' share would surely be larger if covered bonds—bonds that represent a claim on a depository institution but that also have specific mortgages as collateral—became more prevalent in the United States.[38] The mortgages that depositories are likely to hold in their portfolios would include ARMs and nonstandard mortgages that a depository's loan officer believes to be a good credit risk (because of "soft" information about the borrower that convinces the loan officer that the borrower is a good risk but may be difficult to convey in a standardized form to the securitization markets). Also, without the GSEs' special advantages, depository institutions should find it worthwhile to hold more mortgages that previously would have been sold to the GSEs.

Private-Label Securitization

PRIVATE-LABEL SECURITIZATION WAS MBS securitization by private-sector entities that were not Fannie Mae or Freddie Mac or did not have a guarantee from Ginnie Mae. Prior to and alongside the explosion of subprime mortgage securitization in the 2000s, private-label securities (PLS) were a small but important part of the overall securitization market. PLS were composed of prime jumbo mortgages: high-quality mortgages that were larger in value than the conforming loan limits that applied to the GSEs.[39] The implosion of subprime securitizations in 2007 and 2008 brought down all private-label mortgage-backed securities (PLMBS) with them.

The GSEs and Ginnie Mae securitizations have expanded to fill the breach so that more than 90 percent of recent originations have been sold to the GSEs or securitized with a Ginnie Mae guarantee.[40] But with the GSEs and Ginnie Mae having filled the breach, it is now hard for the PLMBS market to reestablish itself. In essence, the PLMBS (and also depository originate-and-hold transactions) have been crowded out of the market by the expanded presence of the GSEs and Ginnie Mae (and their lower MBS yields and correspondingly lower mortgage costs that accompany their government guarantees). In addition, initial uncertainties about what the final financial reform legislative package would look like (and how it would affect securitization) and continuing uncertainties about the detailed regulations that are authorized by the Dodd-Frank Act of 2010 have also inhibited the possibility of a revived PLMBS effort.

Nevertheless, it is worth considering what the possibilities would be in a more stable environment, in the absence of the GSEs and with a limited role for Ginnie Mae as the securitizer of FHA and VA mortgages. In that stable environment, PLMBS should revive to fill the void. It is likely that the tranching structure described earlier would be used to create a class of relatively safe securities and a class of first-loss (riskier) securities. There are at least two important categories of institutional investors—life insurance companies and pension funds, both of which have long-lived liabilities—that would be natural customers for the long-lived assets (probably in the senior tranches) that would be securitized from 30-year FRMs. Therefore, it seems quite likely that the 30-year FRM would remain the staple of the American residential-mortgage market.[41] Hedge funds and high-risk bond mutual funds would likely be the customers for the more junior tranches. Alternatively, it is possible that private mortgage bond insurers would be interested in offering insurance on some or all of the PLMBS tranches. Furthermore, the credit-default swap market might be a means for investors in PLMBS to reduce their risks.

Given the trauma caused by the subprime securitization collapse, one would expect investors initially to be quite cautious. Tranching structures would likely be relatively simple, and a great deal of information would be required and provided.[42] PLMBS with higher-quality underlying collateral would have larger senior tranches and smaller protective junior tranches; PLMBS with lower-quality collateral would have smaller senior tranches and larger junior tranches. Creditworthiness advisory services would surely be employed.

The general level of mortgage interest rates would be higher than it has been during the GSEs' reign. This increase is an unavoidable consequence of replacing the GSEs—and their unpriced government guarantees—with a private-sector alternative. However, the increase is not likely to be large. The pre-crisis consensus of estimates for the GSEs' effects in keeping mortgage interest rates low—which were largely driven by data that compared the mortgage rates on conforming loans with the rates on otherwise similar jumbo loans—placed that differential at about 25 basis points (0.25 percentage points).[43] This differential seems to be a reasonable estimate of the net increase in a post-crisis environment.

Further, given the presence of widespread subsidies for the consumption and construction of housing, especially through the income tax code, a reduction in the subsidy that occurs directly through housing finance would be an economically sensible move toward a more efficient allocation of the nation's resources.

How to Get from Here to There

As discussed, PLMBS and depository institutions have largely been crowded out in the current environment by the GSEs and Ginnie Mae. Unless something changes, this crowding out will persist.

There are two clear paths to "crowding in" (that is, reducing the crowding out of) the private sector. These two paths are not mutually exclusive:[44]

1. Reduce the GSEs' conforming loan limits.[45] A schedule of annual reductions—say 10 percent per year—should be established to gradually increase the range of jumbo mortgages that would be out of the GSEs' domain and within the domain of PLMBS and depository institutions.

2. Increase the GSEs' guarantee fees.[46] The GSEs have typically charged about 20–25 basis points (0.20–0.25 percentage points) per year on the unpaid principal balance of their MBS in return for the guarantee against credit risk that they provide to their MBS investors. A schedule of annual increases on new MBS—say, 5 basis points per year—should be established. As the guarantee fee increases, the GSE MBS would be less attractive to investors, which would open opportunities for PLMBS and depository institutions. A fee increase would also have the advantage of, in the interim, earning a bit more income for the GSEs and thus reducing the burden that will eventually have to be absorbed by taxpayers.

An Alternative Approach with a Side-by-Side Government Guarantee

THERE APPEARS TO be a widespread belief that a private residential-mortgage finance system may not be viable and that some form of government guarantee for mortgages is necessary. The earlier discussion argues otherwise. Nevertheless, it is worth considering what a government guarantee system—if that is the chosen policy route—ought to look like.

The prominent proposals appear to involve a system of private guarantees that would be provided on MBS,[47] with the federal government providing "catastrophic" or "tail-risk"[48] insurance in the event that a private guarantor fails and cannot honor its guarantees.[49] The federal government would charge an appropriate price for this backup insurance.

As compared with the current GSE system, these proposals have a clear set of advantages: the government guarantee would be explicit; it would be priced; it would be on-budget; and it would apply only to the MBS and not to the private guarantors (or to the nonmortgage obligations of the guarantors).[50] If one believes that in the event of another mortgage crisis, the federal government would inevitably come to the rescue, at least the government will have received the guarantee fee revenue in return for its eventual rescue actions.[51]

However, this proposal has a major drawback: the pricing of the government guarantee. There would be no market or other transparent basis for pricing the guarantee. The political pressures for the government to underprice this tail-risk guarantee would surely be substantial.[52] The pricing problem would be even worse if there were multiple classes of securities (with varying qualities of underlying mortgages) that carried government guarantees. Underpricing would become a renewed vehicle for government subsidization of mortgage borrowing.[53]

As an alternative, consider the following:[54] The federal government would offer side-by-side insurance alongside private MBS guarantors.[55] Its initial ratio might be 25 percent private and 75 percent government.[56] The guarantee would apply only to MBS that had prime mortgages (that is, those that had a 20 percent down payment, suitably high FICO scores, and suitably low housing cost–to–income ratios) as collateral; also, it would not be mandatory.[57] The crucial point of this arrangement is the following: The pricing of the government portion of the MBS guarantee would be entirely passive and would match the private guarantors' pricing. Thus, the pricing of the government guarantee would be market-driven.

A second advantage to this approach is that it has a natural path toward the private system discussed earlier: If the capital and other resources to support the private guarantor function prove strong, the government percentage can be reduced over time with the eventual goal of establishing a private system.[58]

CONCLUSION

THE GSE SYSTEM of residential-mortgage finance is clearly broken. What will replace it remains an unanswered question.

This chapter has laid out the argument for a mortgage-finance system that would rely on private markets. It has also offered an alternative proposal for a side-by-side government guarantee that would be superior to the tail-risk proposals currently circulating.

Under either approach, residential-mortgage finance would be a well-functioning system. Grass would not grow in the streets of America. But grass would continue to grow in the backyards of America.

NOTES

1. The $5 trillion refers to the approximate total value of the mortgages on the GSEs' balance sheets and the mortgages that are the collateral for the mortgage-backed securities that they have issued and guaranteed. As of year-end 2009, the actual value was slightly higher: $5.283 trillion; see Federal Housing Finance Agency, *Report to Congress*, 2009 (Washington, DC, 2010), 131, 148. The Obama administration's report on the future of mortgage finance, delivered February 11, 2011, did not offer a specific proposal but instead outlined three possibilities; see U.S. Department of the Treasury and U.S. Department of Housing and Urban Development (HUD), "Reforming America's Housing Finance Market: A Report to Congress," February 11, 2011, http://www.treasury.gov/initiatives/Documents/Reforming%20America%27s%20Housing%20Finance%20Market.pdf.

2. This chapter focuses on single-family residential mortgages (and not multi-family mortgages), since they constitute the bulk of the GSEs' business. For example, at the end of 2009, only 6.2 percent of the mortgages and mortgage-related assets that Fannie Mae held or had securitized involved multifamily housing; for Freddie Mac, the number was 7.4 percent.

3. This proposal is drawn from Viral V. Acharya et al., *Guaranteed to Fail: Fannie Mae, Freddie Mac and the Debacle of Mortgage Finance* (Princeton: Princeton University Press, 2011), 8.

4. This section draws heavily on W. Scott Frame and Lawrence J. White, "The Industrial Organization of the U.S. Single-Family Residential Mortgage Market,"in *The International Encyclopedia of Housing and Home*, ed. Anthony Sanders, Gregory Scruggs, and Susan Wachter, (New York: Elsevier, forthcoming), http://web-docs.stern.nyu.edu/old_web/economics/docs/workingpapers/2010/Frame,%20White_The%20Industrial%20Organization%20of%20the%20U.S.%20Single-Family%20Residential%20Mortgage%20Industry.pdf.

5. This collateralized arrangement stands in contrast to a personal loan or credit card loan, where there is no collateral. If the mortgage lender also has recourse to the borrower's other assets, this recourse fallback would further reduce the risk to the lender.

6. The net buffer that protects the lender is also affected by the size of the transactions costs that the lender would incur in foreclosing and gaining possession of the house in the event of a borrower default.

7. Reputational costs may also influence the borrower's likelihood of defaulting and thus influence credit risk. For example, if there is considerable social stigma attached to defaulting or the impairment of the borrower's credit score is an important negative consequence of a default, then defaults will be less likely.

8. Negative equity arises when the house is worth less than the outstanding amount that the borrower owes on the mortgage. This is also described as being "under water" or (by real estate agents) "upside down." With a longer term, there are more opportunities for adverse events that could cause the borrower to default.

9. Included in the lender's concern about other debt obligations would be whether the borrower is taking out a second mortgage to fund the down payment (or takes out a second mortgage after the first mortgage has been issued). Although the second mortgage ranks behind the first mortgage in seniority, and thus the first mortgage lender is still buffered against a fall in house value, the owner's smaller equity position (as well as the debt payments that must go toward the second mortgage) increases the likelihood of default (and of the delays and deadweight costs that accompany a default).

10. The borrower's other assets are partly an indication of the borrower's net worth and ability to liquidate assets if the household experiences a negative income shock that would otherwise make the monthly mortgage payment a strain. The other assets may also be important in the event of a default if the lender is legally able to make claims (i.e., has recourse) against those assets.

11. For example, the borrower may have private knowledge of prospective changes in household employment that might affect repayment.

12. In practice, lenders often place floors and ceilings on how much the interest rate on the loan can change within a given time period, so the borrower bears less of the interest-rate risk and the lender bears more. Furthermore, the interest rate on an ARM is usually fixed at a rate that is lower than the market rate for an initial term (commonly five years).

13. Jaffee estimates that the presence of a "free" prepayment option in a 30-year FRM causes lenders to charge an interest rate that is 50 basis points (0.5 percentage points) higher than would otherwise be the case. See Dwight M. Jaffee, "Reforming the Mortgage Market through Private Incentives" (paper, "Past, Present, and Future of the Government Sponsored Enterprises,"

Federal Reserve Bank of St. Louis, November 17, 2010), 23, http://research.stlouisfed.org/conferences/gse/Jaffee.pdf.

14. And, again, the mortgage's interest rate will be higher.

15. In some instances, if the originator was large enough and had the expertise, it might also be the packager.

16. The simplest of these securities are described as "pass-through" securities, whereby the interest and principal repayments of the mortgage borrowers are passed through to the investors (resulting in fewer expenses and fees).

17. Thus, as both a conceptual and a terminological matter, in the vertically disintegrated securitization model, the originators are generally different from the lenders.

18. That is, the risk that an individual mortgage may be atypical and may default and yield a loss for the lender even though most mortgages are creditworthy.

19. Although the traditional model involved the depository institution's holding many mortgages and thus getting the benefit of the law of large numbers, the prevailing legal limitations on the geographic locations of U.S. depository institutions prior to the 1990s meant that most depository institutions were locally oriented and thus were subject to the adverse effects of local economic shocks.

20. It is surely no accident that the first issuance of residential MBS in 1970 carried the guarantee of Ginnie Mae.

21. Again, it was probably no accident that Freddie Mac was a fast second in issuing residential MBS in 1971. Fannie Mae's first issuance of MBS was in 1981.

22. For an overview, see W. Scott Frame and Lawrence J. White, "Fussing and Fuming over Fannie and Freddie: How Much Smoke, How Much Fire?" *Journal of Economic Perspectives* 19 (Spring 2005): 159–84; for an updated picture, see Acharya et al., *Guaranteed to Fail*.

23. The U.S. Treasury has had to supply approximately $160 billion as a capital contribution to cover the negative net worths of the two GSEs, and this sum is likely to rise to at least $200 billion and perhaps even $400 billion.

24. In practice, there are almost always more tranches, with a graduated seniority structure, so that the lower tranches bear greater risk and the higher tranches bear less. With tranching, the securities no longer have a simple pass-through structure. The weighted average of the interest rates paid to the junior and senior securities will roughly equal the interest that the overall pass-through security would carry (which, in turn, roughly equals the average interest rate on the underlying mortgages, minus any fees or expenses).

25. Also, if the securitizer itself were to retain the junior security, this retention would provide even greater assurance to the investors in the senior security. It would indicate that the securitizer (who, presumably, knows more

about the characteristics of the underlying mortgages than does the investor) believes that the quality of the underlying mortgages is high.

26. Of course, if the advice that the advisory services provide is flawed—specifically, if that advice is excessively optimistic as to the creditworthiness of the MBS—then the investors will be exposed to greater credit risk than they had expected. For a discussion of the specific problems of the major U.S. credit-rating agencies, see Lawrence J. White, "Markets: The Credit Rating Agencies," *Journal of Economic Perspectives* 24 (Spring 2010): 211–26.

27. In essence, the S&Ls were "borrowing short" (that is, funding themselves through short-term deposits) and "lending long" (originating and holding 30-year FRMs). Although interest-rate risk was the initial source of difficulties for the S&L industry, it was the "old fashioned" credit risk (and inadequate prudential regulation) of the industry's subsequent investments that ultimately caused the S&L debacle of the late 1980s and early 1990s. For further discussion, see Lawrence J. White, *The S&L Debacle: Public Policy Lessons for Bank and Thrift Regulation* (New York: Oxford University Press, 1991).

28. For example, the cash flows could be structured so that some security holders would receive a more even flow of payments while the holders of counterpart securities would receive a correspondingly more erratic pattern of payments.

29. As was noted above, Jaffee, "Reforming the Mortgage Market through Private Incentives," estimates that the absence of prepayment fees on standard U.S. FRMs adds about 50 basis points (0.5 percentage points) to residential mortgage interest rates.

30. In addition, there could be programs that directly encourage people to become more involved with community governance, regardless of their ownership status.

31. As a more general matter, housing policy should not be relying on incentives such as the income-tax deductibility of mortgage interest expenses by owner-occupiers. This tax incentive encourages households to borrow more than they otherwise would and thus to purchase more house (and more land) than they otherwise would. Such incentives also encourage excessive leveraging and the extraction of equity from housing, which makes homeowners more prone to default on their mortgages. Similarly, exempting owner-occupiers from capital gains taxes on the sale of a primary residence encourages investment in excessively large houses on excessively large lots.

32. Greater detail can be found in Lawrence J. White, "Preventing Bubbles: What Role for Financial Regulation?" *Cato Journal* 31 (Fall 2011): 603–618.

33. Mark Zandi, "Systemic Risk: Are Some Institutions Too Big to Fail, and If So, What Should We Do about It?" Testimony before the Financial Services Committee, U.S. House of Representatives, July 21, 2009.

34. The system described in this section approximates option 1 in Treasury and HUD, "Reforming America's Housing Finance Market," 27.

35. I use the term "largely" rather than "wholly" because FHA/VA mortgage insurance and Ginnie Mae guarantees on their securitizations are likely to remain, but the FHA should be more directly focused on low- and moderate-income households, to encourage them to become first-time homeowners. Many European countries have been able to maintain largely private residential-mortgage finance systems and maintain higher rates of homeownership than the United States; see Jaffee, "Reforming the Mortgage Market through Private Incentives," and Acharya, et al., *Guaranteed to Fail*, ch. 8.

36. These data are from the Federal Reserve's "Flow of Funds"; for more detail, see Frame and White, "The Industrial Organization of the U.S. Residential Mortgage Market." This 30 percent encompasses depository institutions' holdings of "whole loan" mortgages and does not include their holdings of MBS.

37. The last capital advantage for the GSEs was that the total capital that needed to be held for mortgages that became MBS and were bought by banks was only 2.05 percent (0.45 + 1.6). This situation illustrates an important point for prudential regulation: capital requirements for similar instruments need to be set similarly across the array of prudentially regulated financial institutions. Otherwise, like water flowing downhill, mortgages will flow to where the capital requirements are the lowest (that is, where they can be leveraged to the greatest extent).

38. Covered bonds are widely used in Europe. This kind of structure is familiar in the U.S. market in the form of repurchase agreements (repos) and advances (loans) to depository institutions from the Federal Home Loan Bank System. For further discussion of covered bonds, see Frank Packer, Ryan Stever, and Christian Upper, "The Covered Bond Market," *BIS Quarterly Review* (September 2007): 43–55. As this paper will discuss later, life insurance companies and pension funds—as issuers of long-lived liabilities—are natural customers for the long-lived assets that arise from 30-year FRMs. Covered bonds (in addition to the senior tranches of private-label securitizations) may be another financial instrument that attracts those categories of investors to these assets.

39. As of year-end 2000, before the mushrooming of subprime securitization, the private-label MBS outstanding totaled $385.5 billion. This total was approximately 13 percent of all outstanding MBS, plus mortgages held in portfolio by the GSEs.

40. See Treasury and HUD, "Reforming America's Housing Finance Market." Aiding that expansion has been the expansion of the conforming loan limit for the GSEs in high housing cost areas. Whereas the conforming loan limit was

generally $417,000 in 2007 (and it remains at that level in most areas), it was raised in 2008 and again in 2009 for high housing cost areas to amounts as high as $729,750. Similarly, the ceiling on FHA loans (which become securitized with Ginnie Mae guarantees) is as high as $729,750 in high housing cost areas. The median sales price for existing homes in the United States at year-end 2009 was approximately $170,000; the median price of a new home was $226,000. It is clear that the swath of housing that is encompassed by the GSE conforming loan limits and by the FHA ceiling (and is eligible for the subsidy that is embedded in these mortgages) extends far above the range that would usually be described as "middle income housing."

41. However, the appeal of those long-lived PLMBS to these investor classes would likely be enhanced if the lender's interest-rate risk could be reduced through explicit prepayment fees.

42. If, for some reason, there seems to be an institutional barrier to the provision of adequate information for these securitizations, this would be a suitable area for government regulation.

43. For a discussion, see Frame and White, "Fussing and Fuming over Fannie and Freddie."

44. Also, along with the reduction in new business, to which both routes point, the GSEs' portfolios of mortgages should be gradually shrunk.

45. This shrinkage should also apply to FHA loans (and thus Ginnie Mae securitizations), with the goal that the FHA should be focusing on providing assistance to low and moderate-income households to encourage them to become homeowners. This goal would imply substantially lower loan limits than even the $271,050 amount (which is 65 percent of the GSEs' $417,000 conforming loan limit) that applies to FHA loans in areas without high housing costs.

46. This route was recently proposed by John Hempton, "What to Do with Fannie and Freddie," January 24, 2011, http://brontecapital.blogspot.com/2011/01/what-to-do-with-fannie-and-freddie.html.

47. The firms that provide the guarantees would be prudentially regulated, since they are, in essence, insurance companies.

48. "Tail risk" is the risk that apparently unlikely events (events that appear to be "in the tail of the distribution") will occur.

49. See, for example, National Association of Home Builders, "Future of Fannie Mae and Freddie Mac and the Housing Finance System," resolution no. 3, January 18, 2010; National Association of Realtors, "Recommendations for Restructuring the GSEs," 2010, http://www.realtor.org/wps/wcm/connect/430e5f80418e341a9039fda3819af93a/government_affairs_gse_recomm_0810.pdf?MOD=AJPERES&CACHEID=430e5f80418e341a9039fda3819af93a; Financial Services Roundtable, Housing Policy Council, "Moving beyond Fannie Mae and Freddie Mac: A Proposal for a New

Generation of Entities to Facilitate a Secondary Market," February 26, 2010, http://www.fsround.org/housing/pdfs/pdfs2010/MOVINGBEYOND FANNIEMAEANDFREDDIEMAC2-26-10.pdf; Diana Hancock and Wayne Passmore, "An Analysis of Government Guarantees and the Functioning of Asset-Backed Securities Markets," Finance and Economics Discussion Series no. 2010-46, Divisions of Research and Statistics and Monetary Affairs, Federal Reserve Board, 2010, http://www.federalreserve.gov/pubs/feds /2010/201046/201046pap.pdf; Hancock and Passmore, "Catastrophic Mortgage Insurance and the Reform of Fannie Mae and Freddie Mac," (Brookings Conference, "Restructuring the U.S. Residential Mortgage Market," February 11, 2011), http://www.brookings.edu/~/media/Files /events/2011/0211_mortgage_market/0211_reform_fannie_freddie _hancock_passmore.pdf; Toni Dechario et al., "A Private Lender Cooperative Model for Residential Mortgage Finance," Federal Reserve Bank of New York, Staff Report no. 466, August 2010, http://www.ny.frb.org/research/staff _reports/sr466.pdf; Mortgage Bankers Association, "Letter to Timothy F. Geithner and Shaun Donovan," June 17, 2010; Center for American Progress, "A Responsible Market for Housing Finance: A Progressive Plan to Reform the U.S. Secondary Market for Residential Mortgages," Market Finance Working Group, January 2011, http://www.americanprogress.org/issues/2011/01 /pdf/responsiblemarketforhousingfinance.pdf; Karen Dynan and Ted Gayer, "The Government's Role in the Housing Finance System: Where Do We Go from Here?" (Brookings Conference,"Restructuring the U.S. Residential Mortgage Market, February 11, 2011), http://www.brookings.edu/~/media /Files/rc/papers/2011/0211_housing_finance_dynan_gayer/0211_housing _finance_dynan_gayer.pdf; and Mark Zandi and Cristian de Ritis, "The Future of the Mortgage Finance System," Moody's Analytics, February 7, 2011, http://www.economy.com/mark-zandi/documents/Mortgage-Finance -Reform-020711.pdf. These proposals are the basis for option 3 in Treasury and HUD, "Reforming America's Housing Finance Market," 29. An alternative proposal would bring government guarantees into the picture only at times of general and severe distress in MBS markets, and the guarantees would apply only to new MBS so as to sustain the new supply of housing finance. See David Scharfstein and Adi Sunderam, "The Economics of Housing Finance Reform: Privatizing, Regulating and Backstopping Mortgage Markets," (Brookings Conference, "Restructuring the U.S. Residential Mortgage Market, February 11, 2011), http://www.treasury.gov/initiatives/Documents /Reforming%20America%27s%20Housing%20Finance%20Market.pdf. This last variant appears to be the basis for option 2 in Treasury and HUD, "Reforming America's Housing Finance Market," 28.

50. In addition, almost all of the proposals recognize that government efforts

to promote affordability of housing should be separate programs and should not be wrapped into the government guarantee system.

51. However, as argued earlier, better prudential regulation of (and, especially, higher required capital levels for) the financial sector should greatly diminish the possibilities that future problems in residential-mortgage finance would mushroom into a larger financial and economic crisis like that of 2008–2009.

52. The experience of underpriced, federally provided flood insurance is not an encouraging precedent.

53. With respect to the Scharfstein and Sunderam proposal in "The Economics of Housing Finance Reform," the Federal Reserve already has clear responsibility for dealing with general and severe stress in U.S. financial markets, including MBS markets. A new agency would be duplicative.

54. This proposal is drawn from Acharya et al., *Guaranteed to Fail*, ch. 8.

55. Again, the MBS guarantors would be prudentially regulated.

56. This 25/75 side-by-side arrangement does mean that the MBS would not be completely guaranteed since (despite the presence of prudential regulation) the private guarantor might fail financially and be unable to honor its obligations on all or part of its guarantees (but the government would, of course, honor its 75 percent share of the guarantee). The incompleteness of the guarantee would provide an incentive for MBS investors to choose their guarantor cautiously.

57. The purpose of limiting the government guarantee is to limit the government's exposure and to avoid mortgage categories that might be thin or exotic (that is, where volumes would be low or the mortgage structures unusual) and where the market's pricing might be more likely to go astray.

58. Also, if the government guarantee is limited only to MBS based on conforming loans, the conforming-loan limit could be ratcheted down over time.

THE FUTURE OF FANNIE MAE AND FREDDIE MAC

MICHAEL LEA AND ANTHONY B. SANDERS

FANNIE MAE AND Freddie Mac, two of the government sponsored enterprises (GSEs), are in conservatorship, and taxpayers are on the hook for over $150 billion in losses. Currently, Fannie, Freddie, and the Federal Housing Administration (FHA) have captured the residential-mortgage market with a market share of more than 90 percent in terms of purchasing mortgage loans and insuring mortgage losses. Given that Fannie and Freddie have essentially crowded the private sector out of the secondary mortgage market, can the private sector offer a less costly alternative to Fannie and Freddie that requires far less government involvement in the housing and mortgage markets?

There is nothing unique per se about Fannie and Freddie that the private sector could not provide. Both the GSEs and the private sector have loan-underwriting models, both can purchase loans and create mortgage-backed securities (MBS), and both can offer mortgage insurance. The one attribute that Fannie and Freddie have that the private sector does not is an explicit guarantee from the federal government.

Is this federal government guarantee necessary to

entice investors to purchase MBS? No. The original "gold standard" mortgage of Fannie and Freddie was the conforming loan with 20 percent or greater down payment and good borrower credit. The default rates on these mortgages have always been very low—typically less than 5 percent for 30-year fixed-rate mortgages—as has the loss per default.[1] The private sector can handle that segment of the market through private insurance markets and portfolio lending and will continue to attract interest from the global investment community. The "gold standard" conforming mortgage market does not need a federal government guarantee. If the private sector can replicate Fannie and Freddie's only unique "virtue"—a federal government guarantee—then there is no justification for keeping Fannie and Freddie around either in conservatorship or in their preconservatorship forms. Fannie and Freddie will not be missed, nor will their absence make a difference to the housing market or the economy, particularly if taxpayers are no longer on the hook for further losses.[2]

GOALS OF GSE REFORM: LESS GOVERNMENT, MORE PRIVATE SECTOR

THE GOAL OF GSE reform is to withdraw the government from the mortgage market and let the private sector take over mortgage lending and securitization. But if GSE reform is going to phase out Fannie and Freddie, it needs to identify what the mortgage-lending landscape would look like without them.

The Obama administration has proposed gradually shrinking the housing GSEs (Fannie, Freddie, and the FHA) to a significantly smaller market share, reflecting

FIGURE 1. GSE/FEDERAL HOME LOAN BANK DEBT VERSUS CASE SHILLER INDEX SINCE 1990

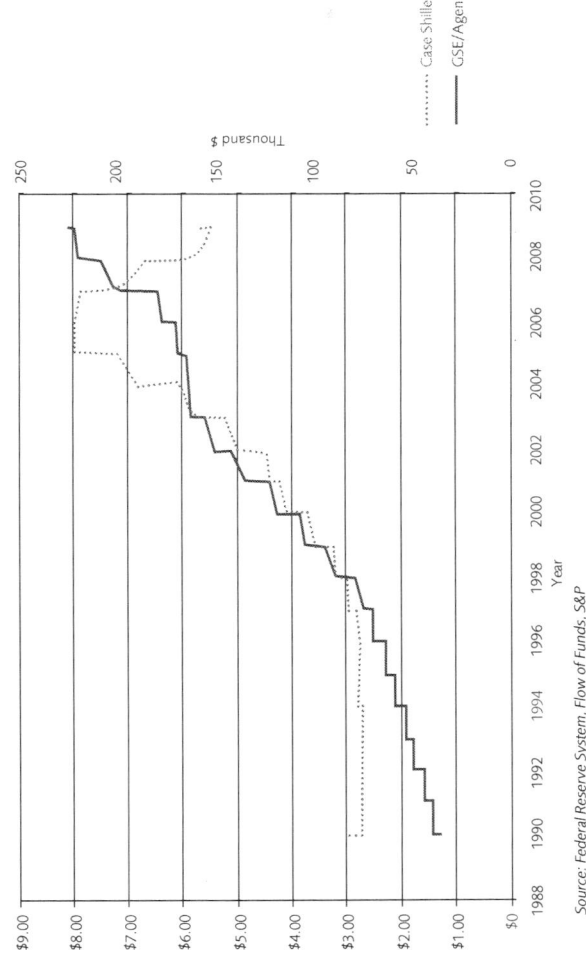

Source: Federal Reserve System, Flow of Funds, S&P

the administration's goal of transitioning away from federally backed mortgage financing.[3] But the housing-reform debate needs to begin with a sober assessment of where the funding of home loans is today. Ninety percent or more of new residential loan originations go into either FHA/Ginnie Mae–, Fannie Mae–, or Freddie Mac–subsidized risk buckets. There is minimal portfolio lending, and private securitizations are nonexistent. Even though the overall mortgage-loan market continues to shrink because of inability of households to qualify for a mortgage, the balance sheets of Fannie and Freddie are growing rapidly, especially with loans held for the portfolio. The largest banks are still selling almost all of the mortgages they originate; at the same time, the banks can purchase the same paper back in the residential mortgage-backed securities (RMBS) market to hold in portfolios to reduce capital requirements.[4] Getting rid of favorable capital treatment for GSEs for banks would stop the capital arbitrage that exists, encouraging banks to hold RMBS.

The first task of housing-finance reform is to find investors who, at some price, would be willing to take the first-loss positions in mortgage loans, held either on balance sheet or in the private RMBS that would replace Fannie and Freddie MBS. If the reformed mortgage markets are able to attract new capital without any change in the funding of the mortgage markets, the size of the mortgage markets will remain the same. However, if some investors are hesitant to hold anything but Fannie and Freddie MBS (because of the guarantee), the mortgage markets will shrink in size. Smaller mortgage markets would be detrimental to the economy, but funding would not evaporate. It would simply be a matter of the price at which investors would supply funds to the mortgage market.

It is clear that the GSEs—along with the FHA and Ginnie Mae—have effectively crowded out the private sector from the residential-mortgage market, capturing over 90 percent market share. Having the government control that large of a segment of the mortgage market is inefficient, and the GSEs are entrenched. Trying to disentangle Fannie and Freddie from the economy will take some work—such as reforming bank capital regulatory rules that prefer the holding of Fannie and Freddie debt. However, disentangling Fannie and Freddie is possible and would eventually eliminate losses to taxpayers.

THE WORLD AFTER FANNIE AND FREDDIE: GOALS FOR HOUSING-MARKET REFORM

THE UNITED STATES is the only major country in the world with GSEs like Fannie Mae and Freddie Mac.[5] Government support of the mortgage market is quite limited in most countries. Only Canada and Japan have a government MBS guarantor, and only Canada and the Netherlands have an FHA equivalent. No other country has experienced the same degree of mortgage-market turmoil as the United States, and many have comparable or higher homeownership rates.

Innovate beyond the 30-Year Fixed-Rate Mortgage

THE UNITED STATES is the only major country in the world with long-term, fixed-rate mortgages as the dominant mortgage product (see Table 1). Even countries such as Germany and Denmark that have traditionally had a high percentage of fixed-rate mortgages have a broader distribution of mortgage products, including long-term, short-term, fixed-rate, and adjustable-rate mortgages. Government backing of securities backed by these mortgages is a major reason for their dominance.

The United States is also unusual in banning or restricting prepayment penalties on fixed-rate mortgages.[6] Most countries allow prepayment penalties to compensate lenders for loss, and interest rates in those countries do not include a significant premium for prepayments, which makes other financing vehicles—such as covered bonds—more common. Even worse, all home buyers in the United States must pay for the option to refinance their 30-year fixed-rate mortgages penalty-free even if they do not want to exercise the option. Hence, the 30-year fixed-rate mortgage is socialized, with everyone paying an interest-rate premium for the option. In Europe, only borrowers who exercise this option pay the cost. U.S. consumers should also be allowed to choose full refinancing, no refinancing, or restricted refinancing of their mortgages.

Finally, the 30-year fixed-rate mortgage exposes lenders and investors to interest-rate risk—along with default risk. Other countries have a greater mix of variable-rate; short-term, fixed-rate; and medium-term, fixed-rate mortgages, which provides their economies—and taxpayers—with less interest-rate exposure. If the United States had a greater variety of mortgages, it would have a more robust housing-finance system.[7] Consumers and regulators should allow mortgage innovation and not simply ban mortgage designs they find "unfriendly."

TABLE 1. INTERNATIONAL MORTGAGE PRODUCT MIX: COMPARISON OF DIFFERENT COUNTRIES AND THEIR MORTGAGE PRODUCTS

Country	Variable Rate (%)	Short-Term Fixed Rate (%)	Medium-Term Fixed Rate (%)	Long-Term Fixed Rate (%)
Australia	92	8	0	0
Canada	35	0	55	10
Denmark	--	17	40	43
France	33	0	0	67
Germany	16	17	38	29
Ireland	91	0	9	0
Japan	38	20	20	22
Korea	92	0	6	2
Netherlands	0	15	66	19
Spain	91	8	0	1
Switzerland	2	0	98	0
United Kingdom	47	53	0	0
United States	5	0	0	95

Source: Michael Lea, International Comparison of Mortgage Product Offerings, *Research Institute for Housing America and Mortgage Bankers Association, 2010.*

Stop Chasing Homeownership

SINCE 1998, FANNIE and Freddie, along with the Department of Housing and Urban Development (HUD), made concerted efforts to increase homeownership rates in the United States. But after the government pumped trillions into the mortgage market through the GSEs (see Figure 1), the homeownership rate is back to around 66 percent (see Figure 2). The government's pursuit of an unsustainable homeownership goal created enormous

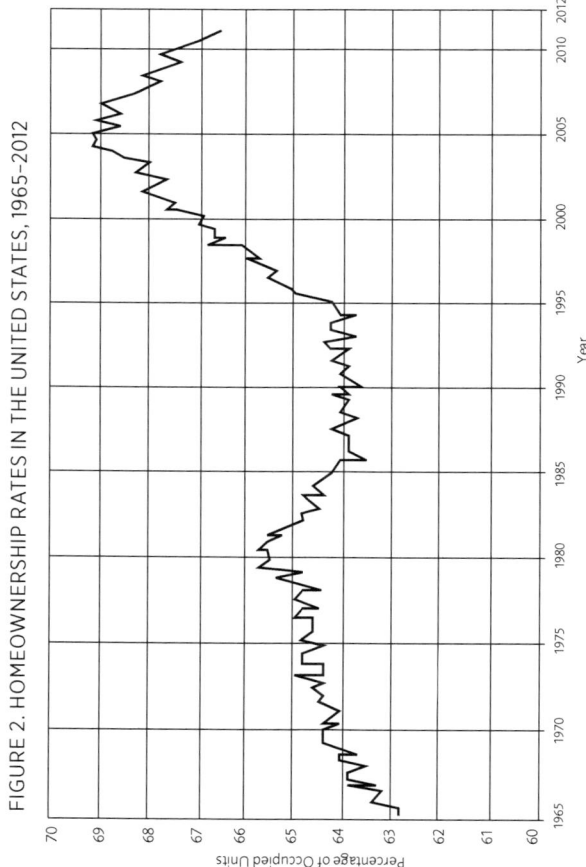

FIGURE 2. HOMEOWNERSHIP RATES IN THE UNITED STATES, 1965–2012

Source: U.S. Census Bureau, "Housing Vacancies and Homeownership," Q 1 2011, http://www.census.gov/hhes/www/housing/hvs/hvs.html.

pain and suffering, all for the sake of increasing homeownership from 66 percent to just over 69 percent.

If we eliminated Fannie and Freddie, would homeownership rates fall further than they already have? As Figure 2 shows, homeownership rates bounced between 63 and 66 percent before GSE funding began to accelerate in 1998.[8] Hence, without Fannie and Freddie in the market, homeownership rates would likely return to the 63–64 percent range. However, if the housing market begins to recover and home prices start to rise again, homeownership rates could actually increase again to around 66 percent.

Our national housing policies pushed too many households into homeownership. Congress and the administration should start unwinding the subsidies to homeownership, starting with Fannie Mae and Freddie Mac.

Reduce the U.S. Mortgage Market's Dependence on Government?

THREE APPROACHES COULD get the private mortgage market back on its feet in a sustainable fashion: (1) covered bonds, (2) a private-label MBS market, and (3) greater lender holding of whole mortgage loans.

Consider Covered Bonds

THE DANISH AND German covered-bond systems have a certain appeal for the U.S. mortgage market. In the German *Pfandbrief* model, covered bonds are securities issued by a bank and backed by a dedicated group of mortgage loans known as a "cover pool."[9] If the issuing bank becomes insolvent, the assets in the cover pool are separated from the issuer's other assets solely for the covered bondholders' benefit.[10] In the Danish system, there is a one-to-one correspondence between a mortgage loan and a mortgage bond (the "balance principle").[11] Under both systems, strict underwriting and loan eligibility standards attempt to minimize loan defaults—just as the Fannie or Freddie conforming loan with a 20 percent or greater down payment was intended to do. Asset eligibility for the cover pool and the process in the event of issuer insolvency are determined by laws specific to each country. Because the credit risk remains on the issuer's balance sheet, the covered-bond system aligns incentives properly.

A critical feature of the *Pfandbrief* and other European covered-bond systems is strict asset and liability matching guidelines that allow funding of mortgages with standardized bonds to govern them.[12] There is no interest-rate risk in the Danish system due to the balance principle that requires strict loan-to-bond matching. One selling point of the German *Pfandbrief* market is that there has never been a default in over 200 years,[13] and no Danish mortgage bank has defaulted on a covered bond.[14]

Revive the Private-Label Mortgage-Backed Securities Market

THE PRIVATE-LABEL MORTGAGE-BACKED securities (PLMBS) market should revive once Fannie and Freddie are not competing with the private sector. The "implied" guarantee for Fannie and Freddie gives them a funding advantage over the private sector,[15] causing them to crowd out the private sector.[16] A number of research papers have found that before Fannie and Freddie were placed in conservatorship, they could have borrowed at rates lower than comparably rated banks.[17]

Once the government removes the implied guarantee from Fannie and Freddie, the PLMBS market should be able to compete with Fannie and Freddie by offering high down-payment prime mortgages. Any proposal requiring government guarantees or credit wraps will allow for continued government control and will not resolve the inefficiencies and misallocations caused by government intervention. The PLMBS market should be allowed to purchase and securitize risky loans as long as bailouts are not allowed.[18]

Increase Portfolio Lending for Banks

BANKS WILL NEED to increase portfolio lending—where they originate the loan and keep it in their portfolio—to supplement covered bonds and securitization. A problem, however, with portfolio lending is the concentration of real-estate assets on bank balance sheets and a declining proportion of deposits. Thus, a significant portion of mortgages will have to be funded in the capital markets with a mixture of (on-balance-sheet) covered bonds and securitization rather than relying on substantial growth in bank portfolio lending.

Privatize Model for Fannie and Freddie

EVEN WITHOUT GOVERNMENT support, Fannie and Freddie have clear franchise value.[19] Once privatized, through the revocation of their charters and the removal of their

Treasury ties, Fannie Mae and Freddie Mac would operate more like nondepository banks or financial institutions. (An assumption behind this approach is that private firms operate more efficiently and expose the taxpayer to less risk.) The operative question is whether the private sector would fund such a model. Maintaining the conduit operations of Fannie and Freddie would facilitate a standardized MBS market that could serve small- to medium-sized lenders. With a clean privatization, the large banks may decide to issue their own securities.

The government could break Fannie and Freddie up into pieces—underwriting platform, securitization operations, research, and so forth—and sell those pieces over a five-year period. Keeping the GSEs in place under alternative forms of ownership would leave the door open to their resurgence in the future.

What about Afforable Housing

CONGRESS NEEDS TO have a serious discussion about how much affordable housing the United States wants and what the cost of affordable housing should be. Because homeownership is risky and very expensive, it is simply not appropriate for all households. The many households that entered the homeownership market when they would have been better off renting have demonstrated this principle. Affordable-housing mandates should be moved from Fannie and Freddie to HUD. Through various programs in both the homeownership and rental markets, HUD and the FHA already support affordable-housing initiatives and could continue to do so.

THE NECESSARY STEPS TO WEANING THE ECONOMY OFF FANNIE AND FREDDIE

THE FIRST STEP to weaning the economy off Fannie and Freddie is to set a five-year "sunset" period during which they cease to exist as government-chartered institutions and transition to the private sector. This transition should be defined by the following steps.

1. Reduce Conforming Loan Limits

FANNIE MAE'S CONFORMING loan limit rose from $207,000 in 1996 to $417,000 in 2006 at the peak of the housing bubble. This increase represents a doubling of the conforming loan limit in a little over 10 years. By 2008, the conforming loan limit had risen to $729,750 in high-cost areas.[20] Higher conforming loan limits—coupled with Fannie and Freddie's guarantee—crowded out the private market, particularly when Fannie and Freddie were capturing the lower-risk mortgage loans and leaving the private markets to insure and securitize the higher-risk mortgage loans.

To crowd out Fannie and Freddie in favor of private markets, the conforming loan limits should be lowered over time. Given a five-year sunset period for Fannie and Freddie, it would be tempting simply to reduce the conforming loan rates by 20 percent per year. This approach has a certain appeal.[21] However, it may also cause turbulence in the housing market if lending ceases. To avoid further rapid declines in home prices that could cause serious damage to the banking industry, the conforming loan limit should be a function of house-price changes. Furthermore, the loan limit should be regionalized to even out the effect of declines in the conforming loan limits.

The first year could be limited to a 10 percent decline in conforming loan limits. At the end of one year, housing prices and the recovery of the private market should be reviewed. If housing prices remain stable and the private sector has begun lending, then another 10 percent decline should be scheduled for the next year, and so on. But it should be made clear that even though the conforming loan rate would return to 50 percent of its current level at the end of the fifth year, Fannie and Freddie would no longer be purchasing or insuring mortgages.

2. Cease the Purchasing of Nonprime, Affordable-Housing Goal Mortgages

DURING THE FIVE-YEAR sunset period, Fannie and Freddie should limit any loan purchases to prime mortgages with sufficient down payments, which has been 20 percent of purchase price or with private mortgage insurance covering the exposure greater than 80 percent loan-to-value. They should not be allowed to purchase nonprime and low down-payment mortgages—or any other mortgage related to affordable-housing goals.

Eliminating affordable-housing goals for Fannie and Freddie is vital to avoiding the purchase of increasingly risky loans. As HUD already sponsors affordable-housing programs, there is no need for Fannie and Freddie to sponsor redundant programs.

3. Freeze and Unwind Retained Portfolios

FANNIE AND FREDDIE'S current retained portfolios should be frozen in terms of new additions and be allowed to unwind and sell off. The retained portfolios should be sold to the Federal Reserve. The Fed can finance this purchase by selling some of its Treasury and MBS holdings, retaining the difference between agency debenture rates and Treasury borrowing costs. Under the Fed's supervision, the portfolios can run off; the Fed may also decide to sell the more liquid loans to investors. This process may take longer than the five-year sunset period for liquidity reasons.

4. Eliminate Nonmortgage Investments

DURING THE FIVE-YEAR sunset period, Fannie and Freddie should not be allowed to invest in nonmortgage investments; they should function as purchasers and securitizers only. This would prevent Fannie and Freddie from accumulating an investment portfolio as well as a retained portfolio. Allowing Fannie and Freddie to purchase nonmortgage investments would be counterproductive to the securitization mission since they would be operating as a financial investor rather than a simple securitizer.

PREDICTED CHANGES FOR LENDERS AND CONSUMERS WITHOUT FANNIE AND FREDDIE

WHAT WOULD HAPPEN to the U.S. mortgage market with only the FHA, covered bonds, and private-label MBS? Quantifying the impact of eliminating Fannie and Freddie is difficult as the United States has not had a period without GSEs since the 1930s. But here is an educated guess of what the residential-mortgage market would look like:

- New mortgage rates would probably be higher, in the range of 50 to 100 basis points (bps)—or 0.5 to 1 percent additional interest rate—in the short term. As a result, home prices would fall slightly or take longer to recover. In the longer term, the rate would be 40–100 bps higher than current rates.[22]

- More short-term fixed and variable-rate mortgages, to the extent that regulations allow them, would exist. In particular, there would be more rollover mortgages, where the borrower's rate changes to the market rate after a fixed period.[23]

- If mortgage rates increased, homeownership rates would be marginally lower, because of higher interest rates.

- Higher down payments would produce safer mortgages for lenders, investors and mortgage insurers.

For lenders, there are two possible outcomes. The first outcome, which seems unlikely, is that the mortgage markets could shrink because investors are unwilling to fund mortgages. The second and more likely outcome is that banks and other entities expand to fill the gap left by Fannie and Freddie.

Without the government guarantee, mortgage rates will rise to attract new capital.[24] Today, there are huge accumulations of capital waiting to reenter the market. The primary obstacle to capital entry is the lack of clarity regarding the government's role in mortgage guarantees and regulation. Once government clarifies its role, private capital will be forthcoming. Over time, alternate capital—such as sovereign wealth funds, foreign central bank holdings, and mutual funds—will enter the market to augment large U.S. funds. Banks are likely to hold more mortgages on balance sheet, funded by a combination of deposits and covered bonds. Correctly structured, PLMBS with large down payments and good credit scores would alleviate some investor concerns, but there is a chance mortgage rates would still have to increase to cover the expected guarantee benefits.

Current mortgage rates for conforming loans are influenced by the economics of the GSEs.[25] The GSEs charged 15–20 bps for their credit guarantee. This was a result of a capital requirement of only 45 bps for sold mortgages and expected losses and operating costs in the neighborhood of single-digit bps.[26] Private guarantors are likely to require significantly more capital. Equity capital is likely to be more in the range of 4–10 percent. This capital might require somewhat lower returns than the 25 percent return on equity the GSEs were able to obtain but is not likely to be much below 15 percent on the first 5 percent of capital. This requirement creates a minimum capital charge of 75 bps plus any amounts required to cover expected losses and operating costs. These "advantages" of the GSEs relative to private funding must be weighed against the fact that they operated at noncompetitive and extremely low levels of capital that are not sustainable.

CONCLUSION

FANNIE MAE AND Freddie Mac should be phased out over a five-year period. Covered bonds—like those used in Denmark and Germany—and an improved PLMBS market should take their place, along with an increase in lender-portfolio lending. Without Fannie and Freddie, there may be a small drop in homeownership rates as well as a small increase in mortgage interest rates. In other words, not much will change in a world without Fannie Mae and Freddie Mac, other than saving taxpayers hundreds of billions of dollars in the future.

NOTES

1. Frank Northaft, "What's Driving Mortgage Delinquencies?" Freddiemac.com, March 22, 2010, http://www.freddiemac.com/news/blog/frank_nothaft/20100322_what_drives_mortgage_delinquencies.html.
2. To be sure, affordable-housing groups and the housing industry would prefer to have an explicit guarantee because they believe mortgage rates are lower when the government guarantees mortgages.
3. Prime Alliance, "The Treasury's Proposal for GSE Reform," 2011, http://www.primealliancesolutions.com/rc-press-releases/189-the-treasurys-proposal-for-gse-reform.
4. Mortgage loans have a 4 percent capital requirement, whereas Fannie Mae and Freddie Mac securities have only a 1.6 percent capital requirement.
5. Michael Lea, "Alternative Forms of Mortgage Finance: What Can We Learn from Other Countries?" in *Moving Forward: The Future of Consumer Credit and Mortgage Finance*, ed. Nicolas Retsinas and Eric Belsky, (Washington, DC, and Cambridge, MA: Brookings Institution Press and Joint Center for Housing Studies, 2011).
6. Approximately half of the states have prohibitions on prepayment penalties on fixed-rate mortgages. Perhaps more importantly, Fannie and Freddie have stated that they would not honor prepayment penalties on any fixed-rate mortgages they purchase; see Lea and Sanders, "Do We Need the 30-Year Fixed-Rate Mortgage?" (working paper, Mercatus Center at George Mason University, Arlington, VA, 2011).
7. There is a danger that the Dodd-Frank definition of a "qualified residential mortgage" will further ensconce the fixed-rate mortgage as the dominant instrument; see Michael Lea, "International Comparison of Mortgage Product Offerings," (special report, Research Institute for Housing America,

September 2011).

8. Business Wire, "Celebrating All-Time Record Homeownership Rate of 66.8 Percent. Fannie Mae's Johnson Challenges Mortgage Industry to Strive for 68 Percent Homeownership by End of Decade," bnet.com, October 23, 1998, http://findarticles.com/p/articles/mi_m0EIN/is_1998_Oct_23/ai_53118862.

9. *Pfandbrief* is the trademark name for the German covered bond. In the Pfandbrief model, a pool of qualifying mortgages backs the securities.

10. The Federal Deposit Insurance Corporation (FDIC) is concerned about covered bonds and overcollateralization (OC). The solution to the FDIC's concern is to limit OC. Tight asset-liability matching leads to the lowest OC requirements and aligns sovereign deposit guarantors with legislated covered bonds.

11. For more information on European covered bonds, see European Covered Bond Council, "European Covered Bond Factbook," September 2010, http://www.law.berkeley.edu/files/bclbe/European_Covered_Bond_Factbook_2010.pdf. For more information on the Danish system, see Unicredit Global Credit Research, "Danish Covered Bonds—A Primer," August 2008, http://www.nykredit.dk/investorcom/ressourcer/dokumenter/pdf/SR080608_DanishCoveredBonds.pdf.

12. Some covered-bond issuers have failed due to interest-rate risk in Germany. The resolution has been a merger with a solvent bank and subsequent tightening of asset- and liability-matching requirements.

13. This selling point is a little misleading since Germany has had several episodes of hyperinflation. While there has not been a default per se, hyperinflation has caused the payment stream to become virtually worthless at times; see Moody's Global Credit Research, "Structured Finance in Focus: A Short Guide to Covered Bonds," May 2010.

14. This lack of default is not to be confused with banks failing. Recently, Denmark has experienced several bank failures; see Unicredit Global Credit Research, "Danish Covered Bonds—A Primer."

15. Note that the private-label commercial mortgage-backed securities (CMBS) market has revived itself without any government guarantee—implicit or explicit.

16. The continued uncertainty about the accounting and regulatory treatment of private-label securities is also a barrier to a revival of the market. Issues surrounding true sale, risk retention, and reporting need to be resolved before the market can expand.

17. Brent W. Ambrose and Arthur Warga, "Implications of Privatization: The Costs to Fannie Mae and Freddie Mac," *Studies on Privatizing Fannie Mae and Freddie Mac* (Washington, DC: HUD, May 1996); and Anthony B. Sanders,

"Government Sponsored Agencies: Do the Benefits Outweigh the Costs?" *Journal of Real Estate Economics* 25 (2002): 121–127.

18. Fannie Mae, "2011 Single-Family Mortgage Loan Limits," January 11, 2011, http://www.fanniemae.com/aboutfm/loanlimits.jhtml.

19. Their franchise value lies in their business operations, including systems and business relationships with lenders and investors, an incomparable database for analyzing risk, and master servicing. While these characteristics can be replicated to a degree in the private market, it would be a while before a private entity could achieve similar scale and economies. This situation does beg a question about market dominance that may need to be addressed by regulation.

20. Fannie Mae, "2011 Single-Family Mortgage Loan Limits."

21. Making the phaseout of the conforming loan limits clear would force the private sector to brace for a world without Fannie and Freddie. Alternatively, taking the loan limits down to late-1980s levels ($175,000) and then selling them off in the private sector would prevent an overly rapid removal of the guarantee effects.

22. Mercatus Center estimates are similar to those found in Andrew Davidson and Eknath Belbase, "Imagining No GSEs: The Potential Impact of Dismantling Fannie and Freddie," *Pipeline*, no. 94 (February 2011).

23. Rollover mortgages are common in Canada. They are similar to the 30-year fixed-rate mortgage, but are fixed for only a limited time, such as five years, with a longer amortization period. At the end of every five years, the loan rate is renegotiated.

24. Mortgage rates will likely rise, even if GSE status is continued, if significantly higher capital requirements are imposed.

25. See Davidson and Belbase, "Imagining No GSEs: The Potential Impact of Dismantling Fannie and Freddie."

26. It is clear from Fannie and Freddie's losses that they greatly underpriced their guarantee, leading to massive taxpayer losses.

DO WE NEED THE 30-YEAR FIXED-RATE MORTGAGE?

MICHAEL LEA AND ANTHONY B. SANDERS

A CENTRAL ARGUMENT in the ongoing discussion about the fates of Fannie Mae and Freddie Mac is the importance of the 30-year, fixed-rate, prepayable mortgage (hereafter referred to as the FRM). David Min asserts that the FRM is an *essential* part of the U.S. housing-finance system.[1] Susan Woodard emphasizes the *special role* of the FRM, stating, "Americans now seem to regard the availability of long-term fixed-rate mortgages as part of their civil rights."[2] Adam Levitin and Susan Wachter assert that the FRM is *critical* for sustainable homeownership.[3] All four analysts advocate continued government support of Fannie Mae and Freddie Mac in order to preserve the FRM.

The FRM occupies a central role in the U.S. housing-finance system. The dominant instrument since the Great Depression, the FRM currently accounts for more than 90 percent of mortgage originations. One reason it enjoys enduring popularity is that the FRM is a consumer-friendly instrument. Not only does the FRM offer payment stability, the instrument also provides a one-sided bet in borrowers' favor. If rates rise, borrowers benefit from a below-market interest rate. If rates fall, borrowers can benefit from exercising the prepayment option in the FRM to lower their mortgage interest rates.

But these consumer benefits have costs. It is costly to provide a fixed, nominal interest rate for as long as 30 years. And the prepayment option creates significant costs. If rates rise, the lender has a below-market-rate asset on its books. If rates fall, the lender again loses as the mortgage is replaced by another with a lower interest rate. To compensate for this risk, lenders incorporate a premium in mortgage rates that all borrowers pay regardless of whether they benefit from refinance. Exercise of the prepayment option in the contract also has significant transactions costs for the borrower and imposes additional operating costs on the mortgage industry.

Another major reason for the FRM's dominance is government support and regulatory favoritism. The FRM is subsidized through the securitization activities of Fannie Mae, Freddie Mac, and Ginnie Mae. Their securities benefit from a government guarantee that lowers the relative cost of the instrument, which is their core product. These guarantees have a significant cost as the government backing of Fannie Mae and Freddie Mac has exposed taxpayers to large losses.

Are the FRM's benefits worth its costs? Would the FRM disappear if Fannie and Freddie stopped financing it? Are there mortgage alternatives that balance the needs of consumers and investors without exposing the taxpayer to inordinate risk? This chapter seeks to answer these questions, starting with a brief history of the FRM and emphasizing the government's ongoing role in enhancing its presence. The chapter then discusses the

FRM's benefits and costs to consumers, investors, taxpayers, and the economy and ends with a depiction of a world in which Fannie Mae and Freddie Mac no longer support the FRM.

THE FRM: A BRIEF HISTORY

THE FRM HAS been the dominant instrument throughout the post-Depression period. Prior to the Depression, the standard mortgage instrument was a five to ten year, fixed-rate, nonamortizing loan that required borrowers to refinance or repay the loan at the end of its term. Then, in 1934, the Federal Housing Administration (FHA) effectively created the FRM with the National Housing Act, which authorized the FHA as a mutual insurance company providing mortgage insurance on specific mortgage types.[4] The original FHA mortgage had the following features:

- It was fully amortizing with a fixed, annual-contract interest rate of 5.5 percent.

- It required a minimum down payment of 20 percent of the property's appraised value.

- Its maximum term was 20 years.

- Its maximum loan amount was $16,000.

- It was freely assumable.

- It had no prepayment penalty.[5]

Over time the maximum term and loan amount have increased, and FRMs have become due on sale.

Government policy supported the FRM from its inception. Fannie Mae (initially the Federal National Mortgage Association) was created as a government agency in 1938 to purchase FHA mortgages. FHA- and later Veteran's Affairs (VA)-insured mortgages were the dominant instruments until the 1960s. The government insurers administratively set rates that made it difficult for noninsured loans to compete with government-insured instruments.[6] Federally insured savings and loan institutions (S&Ls) were restricted to offering only FRMs until 1981.[7]

Ginnie Mae, also a government agency, was created in 1968 to liquidate the subsidized portfolio held by Fannie Mae, which was privatized in that year. Ginnie Mae developed the mortgage-backed security to facilitate liquidation. Ginnie Mae began guaranteeing securitized pools of FHA- and VA-insured loans in 1970, providing a full faith and credit, timely payment guarantee facilitating their sale.

The government created Freddie Mac in 1970 to assist S&Ls in managing the interest-rate and liquidity risk inherent to the FRM. Accounting and tax policies in the 1980s that made it easier for S&Ls to sell underwater FRMs without immediately recognizing a loss stimulated the development and growth of the secondary mortgage market.[8] Fannie Mae and Freddie Mac introduced the concept of the "swap" in the 1980s that allowed lenders to exchange their portfolios of FRMs for securities with lower capital requirements, reducing the cost of holding the loans. The large-scale sale of

FRMs increased liquidity in fixed-rate mortgage securities, leading to improved pricing. The timely payment guarantees on mortgage securities provided by Ginnie Mae, Fannie Mae, and Freddie Mac lowered the relative price of securities backed by conforming fixed-rate loans, increasing the instrument's market share.[9]

The prepayment feature is a key factor in the FRM's dominance. FRMs contain an embedded option for borrowers to prepay their loans without penalty. Government policy promotes this feature: many states ban prepayment penalties on FRMs, and Fannie Mae and Freddie Mac will not enforce a prepayment penalty on FRMs they purchase.[10]

Adjustable-rate mortgages (ARMs) were introduced by state-chartered S&Ls in the 1960s and allowed by regulation for federally chartered institutions in 1981. Since that time, the FRM's market share has fluctuated based on the level and direction of interest rates. ARMs have achieved a market share as high as 35 percent for some short periods (when the FRM-ARM spread is wide or rising), but for the most part have had a market share of 20 percent or less.[11] While Fannie Mae, Freddie Mac, and the FHA have introduced ARM products, these agencies have directed most of their efforts toward developing and enhancing their fixed-rate offerings. Today, more than 90 percent of mortgage originations are FRMs, reflecting Federal Reserve efforts to keep rates low through monetary policy and quantitative easing and the fact that Fannie Mae, Freddie Mac, and Ginnie Mae are the only funding sources for mortgage loans.

The 2010 Dodd-Frank financial reform bill enshrined the FRM's dominance through the "qualified mortgage."[12]

Lenders will get safe harbor from risk-retention requirements for qualified residential mortgages (QRMs), as well as other regulatory benefits. Lenders will likely make QRMs their loans of choice, relegating non-QRMs to the nonbanking, non-GSE realms of private-market securitizations through private-equity funds, REITs, and other vehicles.

BENEFITS OF FRMs

A LONG HISTORY of government support is not the only reason for the FRM's dominance. The instrument offers consumers several advantages. First and foremost, it provides nominal payment stability, which helps consumers budget and reduces the likelihood of default. The monthly payment on an FRM is the same throughout the life of the loan, whereas borrowers with ARMs can experience payment shock in a volatile interest-rate environment, making them more likely to default.[13] The FRM is also a simple instrument for borrowers to understand, which has led to proposals that lenders be required to offer the instrument to consumers applying for a mortgage.[14]

The option to prepay an FRM without penalty is another consumer advantage.[15] This feature effectively converts the FRM into a downwardly adjustable-rate mortgage. When market interest rates fall, the borrower can refinance into a new loan at a lower rate. When rates rise, the fixed-rate feature protects the borrower against rising mortgage payments. Thus, the FRM (as opposed to a short-term ARM, for example) shields borrowers from most interest-rate risk. But the risk does not disappear—the lower the risk for the borrower, the greater it is for the lender or investor.

COSTS OF FRMs

THE INSTRUMENT'S SUPPORTERS point out that it is easier for investors than consumers to manage interest-rate risk. It is true that lenders and investors have more tools at their disposal to manage interest-rate risk. But managing prepayment risk is costly and difficult and many institutions have suffered significant losses as a result (for example, S&Ls in the 1980s; hedge funds and mortgage companies in the 1990s and 2000s).[16] Furthermore, borrowers rarely stay in the same home or keep the same mortgage for 15–30 years,[17] so one can reasonably ask why rates should be fixed for such long periods (increasing the loan's cost and risk). Also, the taxpayer ultimately bears a significant portion of the risk through support of Fannie Mae and Freddie Mac.

Min argues that the FRM promotes financial- and housing-market stability. A system dominated by ARMs or short-term, fixed-rate mortgages is more sensitive to interest-rate fluctuations than one dominated by the FRM and can contribute to boom–bust cycles in housing. Housing demand is more rapidly influenced by monetary policy with ARMs relative to FRMs. But FRMs hardly eliminate housing cycles. The United States has experienced pronounced housing cycles in most decades since World War II, including a massive housing boom and bust in the last decade. Min attributes the most recent cycle to the rapid growth in short-duration mortgages. In large part, the shortening average life of mortgages reflects the widespread exercise of the FRM prepayment option.

The FRM has a uniquely one-sided design that protects the borrower at the expense of the lender or investor. But such protection comes at a cost. Longer-term, fixed-rate loans have higher rates than shorter-term, fixed-rate loans in most interest-rate environments (Table 1). Having a range of fixed-rate terms allows the borrower to trade off monthly payment stability with overall mortgage affordability. For example, a mortgage whose interest rate is fixed for 30 years will usually have the highest interest rate, while a three-to-one ARM, whose interest rate is fixed only for the first three years, will usually have the lowest interest rate.

TABLE 1. MORTGAGE PRICING

INSTRUMENT	PRICING AT 5/20/2011	
	Rate	Points
30 year FRM	4.5%	-0.5
10 year FRM	3.75%	-0.5
3:1 ARM	2.75%	-0.625
5:1 ARM	2.875%	-0.5
10:1 ARM	3.875%	-0.25

Source: MetLife Home Loan—negative points used to pay closing costs.

Also, prepayable mortgages have higher rates than non-prepayable mortgages. In effect, all U.S. mortgage borrowers pay for the option to refinance regardless of whether they exercise it. This system differs from the Canadian and European systems. In those systems, the borrower receives a short- to medium-term fixed-rate loan without a free prepayment option. If the borrower wants to prepay for financial reasons (as opposed to moving), they must pay a penalty equivalent to the investor's or lender's cost to reinvest the proceeds at the new, lower market rate. The option's cost is thus individualized—borne by the individual exercising the option. In the United States, the option's cost is socialized, with all borrowers paying a premium in their mortgage rates (on average, around 50 basis points, or 0.5 percent).[18] In effect, the prepayment option is a tax on all borrowers.

Because all borrowers pay for the prepayment option, borrowers who do not exercise the option effectively subsidize those who do. Most often, unsophisticated borrowers who are intimidated by the refinance process or who are credit impaired pay the subsidy. The latter group is most likely to benefit at the margin (that is, by lowering the risk of default) but least able to refinance.

Alex J. Pollock points out another significant problem with the FRM.[19] When interest rates and house prices are rising, borrowers benefit from constant nominal and falling real mortgage payments and get to keep the inflation premium in the house price. But if interest rates are low and house prices are falling, a dark side emerges. Borrowers often cannot refinance because of the fall in house prices, and they are stuck with high nominal and real mortgage payments and potential negative equity. As a result, they are unable to take advantage of historically low interest rates. Many borrowers find themselves in this situation today.

The potential for negative equity with a slowly amortizing mortgage product is daunting. For example, Figure 1 shows what would happen with a 30-year, fixed-rate mortgage paydown when house prices are declining by 2.5 percent per month. In this example, the borrower is in negative-equity territory by month 11 since house prices are falling faster than the loan is being paid down. The difference between the loan-balance line and the house-price line illustrates how severe the negative-equity problem

FIGURE 1. HOUSE PRICES AND MORTGAGE LOAN BALANCE ON 30-YEAR FRM:
5 PERCENT DOWN PAYMENT WITH −1/2 PERCENT DECLINE IN HOUSE PRICES PER MONTH

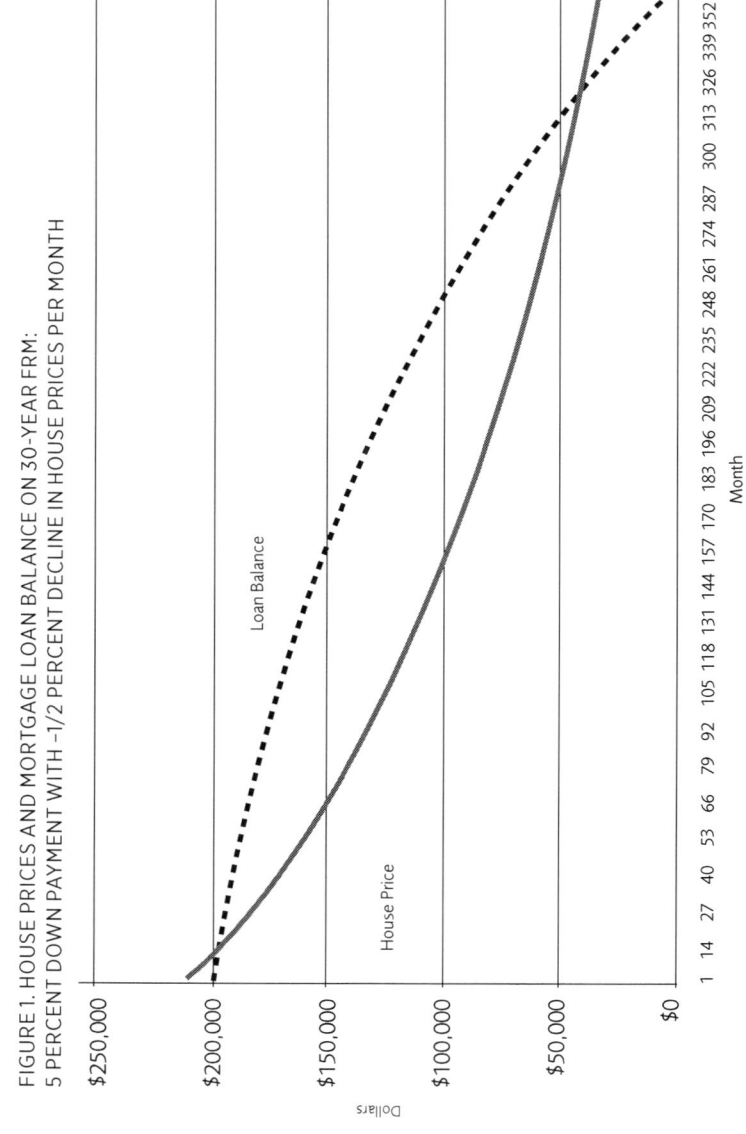

can get with a 30-year, fixed-rate mortgage and declining house prices.

The FRM can create negative equity for borrowers in a rising interest-rate environment as well. When interest rates rise, a house's value may fall and the economic value of the mortgage falls. However, the borrower is still responsible for repaying the loan at par value (the nominal outstanding balance). The combination of falling house price and constant mortgage value can lead to or exacerbate negative equity. Homeowner negative equity can also produce significant economic costs in that homeowners are less likely to move to change their housing consumption or to take advantage of job opportunities.

Rising interest rates cause other problems for FRM borrowers and investors. If rates rise because of expected inflation, FRMs create affordability problems for new borrowers.[20] Unhedged investors experience an economic loss on their holdings of FRM-backed securities when interest rates rise (they also do not benefit from a rate decline, as noted earlier).[21] Rising interest rates also create an extension risk (the risk that the average life of securities rises) for investors. As rates rise, prepayments slow and the effective maturity of the securities increases beyond that expected by investors.[22]

Volatile interest rates cause problems for both borrowers and lenders. Long-term, fixed-rate instruments have greater sensitivity to interest-rate changes than shorter-term instruments do. Volatility in pricing also makes mortgage shopping more difficult for borrowers in that mortgage prices can vary significantly on a daily (or even intraday) basis.[23]

Interest-rate volatility also causes refinancing waves,

FIGURE 2. MORTGAGE REFINANCE VOLUME VERSUS FREDDIE MAC 30-YEAR FIXED RATE MORTGAGE RATE

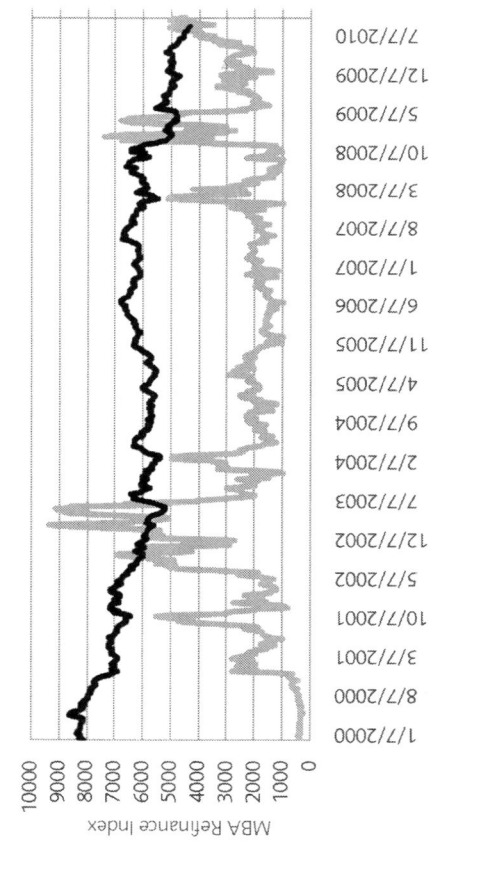

Source: Mortgage Bankers Association.
Note: Refinance Index is nonseasonally adjusted. Base period for index is March 16, 1990 = 100.

which increase costs for mortgage originators and borrowers. As interest rates rise and fall, mortgage origination volume is subject to massive swings. Mortgage originators and servicers have significant costs associated with managing such volatility. For example, origination volume rose from less than $3 trillion in 2002 to nearly $4 trillion in 2003 and fell to less than $3 trillion in 2004 (Figure 2). Thus, the industry had to increase capacity by 33 percent in one year and reduce it by 25 percent the following year. FRM refinancing was the main reason for this volatility. For mortgage borrowers, the cost of refinancing lies in the thousands of dollars they must pay in origination fees simply to lower their mortgage rates.[24]

The FRM has also created significant costs for taxpayers. Until 1981, federally insured depositories were prohibited from offering ARMs. Predictably, when inflation and interest rates rose in the 1970s and early 1980s, reliance on this instrument effectively killed off the S&L industry. In 1982, approximately 80 percent of the S&L industry was bankrupt and insolvent due to the mismatch between FRM assets and the short-term deposits that funded them. A similar mismatch rendered Fannie Mae insolvent. When numerous thrifts eventually failed, the taxpayer picked up a significant tab to restructure the industry.[25]

Learning from the experience, banks and thrifts continued to originate 30-year FRMs, but only if the loans could be sold to Fannie Mae, Freddie Mac, or guaranteed by Ginnie Mae. In other words, banks and thrifts did not retain the interest-rate risk that they created by originating the FRMs. Instead, investors absorbed the risk. As the ultimate risk bearers, private investors attempted to price and manage the risk (with varying degrees of success). The

GSEs hold a significant portion of the FRM inventory,[26] so when interest rates rise, they may suffer large losses that will be borne by taxpayers.

The FRM's popularity and its government backing produce another significant risk for the government. In order to finance the FRM and allocate the interest-rate risk to investors, the government—through FHA insurance and Fannie/Freddie guarantees—absorbs the mortgages' credit risk. Ironically, it was credit risk that led to the failures of Fannie and Freddie in the financial crisis. While part of their losses can be attributed to speculative investments in subprime and Alt-A backed securities (mostly non-fixed-rate mortgages), a significant portion of their losses have come from FRM defaults.[27] The Federal Housing Finance Agency now projects GSE losses to be $220 to $360 billion. A portion of these losses can be attributed to the policy goal of ensuring the FRM's availability through the government's absorption of the credit risk.

THE MYTH OF THE FRM AS A GOLD STANDARD

DAVID MIN OF the Center for American Progress has written that "the 30-year fixed-rate mortgage remains the gold standard for mortgages throughout the world, offering superior stability for both homeowners and financial systems."[28] If this statement is true, why is the United States one of only two countries with this instrument? And why is the United States the country most afflicted by a housing bust? Given the catastrophic conditions of Fannie Mae and Freddie Mac, it is clear that the 30-year fixed-rate mortgage is outright dangerous—not a gold standard. Perhaps his musing should be rewritten to say, "The 30-year, fixed-rate mortgage remains the fool's gold standard for mortgages throughout the United States, offering superior stability for some homeowners and potential catastrophe for U.S. and global financial systems."

The FRM is a unique instrument by international standards. Only one other country, Denmark, has a long-term, fixed-rate, prepayable (without penalty) mortgage.[29] Several other countries have long-term, fixed-rate products (including France, Japan, and Germany), but the typical terms are shorter and prepayment is subject to penalty. Shorter amortization periods benefit both borrowers and lenders because borrowers accumulate equity faster.

A more common fixed-rate instrument is the rollover mortgage, which is the dominant instrument in Canada and several European countries. Its interest rate is typically fixed for up to five years and "rolls" into a new fixed rate at the end of the term. The new rate is negotiated with the lender and is set at market. These loans also have prepayment penalties during the fixed-rate term but allow total repayment without penalty at the end of the term.

Adjustable-rate loans are the dominant instrument in a number of countries, including Australia, Spain, and the United Kingdom. Table 2 shows the types of mortgages available in different countries and how common each product is.

TABLE 2. INTERNATIONAL MORTGAGE PRODUCTS
(market share of instrument by fixed-rate period)

	Adjustable rate	Short-term fixed rate (1-5 yrs.)	Medium-term fixed rate (5-10 yrs.)	Long-term fixed rate (10+ yrs.)
Australia	92%	8%	--	--
Canada	35%	--	55%	10%
Denmark	--	17%	40%	43%
France	33%	--	--	67%
Germany	16%	17%	38%	29%
Ireland	91%	--	9%	--
Japan	38%	20%	20%	22%
Korea	92%	--	6%	2%
Netherlands	--	15%	66%	19%
Spain	91%	8%	--	1%
Switzerland	2%	--	98%	--
United Kingdom	47%	53%	--	--
United States	5%	--	--	95%

Source: Michael Lea, International Comparison of Mortgage Product Offerings (Washington, DC: Research Institute for Housing America and Mortgage Bankers Association, 2010). No entry means negligible market share.

Many countries have had housing booms and busts during the last decade (including Australia, Denmark, Ireland, and Spain). Yet only Ireland has had as severe of a downturn as the United States (Table 3). Min attributes the U.S. housing cycle to a shortening of the duration of mortgages over the past two decades, which caused house prices to become more sensitive to interest rates. Low interest rates and ample credit clearly contributed to the boom. However, throughout the boom period, a majority of loans were in fact fixed-rate loans. Most of the reduction in average mortgage maturity was due to borrowers' exercising the prepayment option in their FRM contracts. Much of the shortening was for cash-out refinances to facilitate consumption at the expense of wealth accumulation. The inability of households to refinance FRMs to reduce negative equity has exacerbated the current crisis as noted above.

TABLE 3. TROUBLED MORTGAGES: WESTERN EUROPE AND THE UNITED STATES

	>3 month arrears	Impaired or Doubtful	Foreclosures	Year
Belgium	0.46%	--	--	2009
Denmark	0.53%	--	--	2009
France	--	0.93%	--	2008
Ireland	3.32%	--	--	2009
Italy	--	3.00%	--	2008
Portugal	1.17%	--	--	2009
Spain	--	3.04%	0.24%	2009
Sweden	--	1.00%	--	2009
United Kingdom	2.44%	--	0.19%	2009
United States—All	9.47%	--	4.58%	2009
United States.—Prime	6.73%	--	3.31%	2009
United States—Subprime	25.26%	--	15.58%	2009

Source: Dwight M. Jaffee, "Reforming the U.S. Mortgage Market Through Private Incentives" (presentation, Past, Present, and Future of the Government Sponsored Enterprises, Federal Reserve Bank of St. Louis, November 17, 2010). No entry means negligible rate.

Min assumes the prepayment option to be free, but it is far from free, as discussed earlier. While only some borrowers will actually utilize the prepayment option, everyone has to pay for it. Fannie Mae and Freddie Mac will purchase only prepayable mortgages, even though nonprepayable mortgages may be in many borrowers' best interests.

CONCLUSION

THE FUNDAMENTAL QUESTION remains: are the benefits of the FRM worth the costs? All borrowers pay a substantial tax—50 basis points or more—for this instrument. Furthermore, taxpayers have absorbed substantial losses to support this instrument, first through the S&Ls and now through Fannie Mae and Freddie Mac. Should the government subject taxpayers to the risk of another catastrophic meltdown to preserve the FRM? Are there alternatives that maintain some of the FRM's benefits while greatly reducing the costs?

If the government abolished Fannie Mae and Freddie Mac, the FRM would not cease to exist. Private-label securitization in the United States and covered bonds in Denmark have funded this instrument in the past and are fully capable of funding it in the future. Investors are sophisticated enough to price both credit risk and interest-rate risk. Conventional wisdom suggests that U.S. investors won't accept both credit risk and interest-rate risk for large volumes of mortgages and the reason is clear: private investors can get the government to absorb the credit risk at a lower cost than would be charged by the private market. The loss experiences of Fannie and Freddie suggest that they were funding mortgages at below-market (risk-adjusted) rates. Without Fannie and Freddie, the FRM would still be offered by lenders, but not at a subsidized rate. The FRM would have a smaller market share, but it would not disappear, as Min asserts. Nor would the only alternative be a short-term ARM as international experience suggests.

What would emerge as the "standard" U.S. mortgage instrument without government support of the FRM? A rollover mortgage similar to that offered in Canada and several European countries is the likely candidate.[30] This instrument offers borrowers short- to medium-term payment stability, and borrowers can manage interest-rate risk by adjusting the fixed-rate term upon renewal. Modern international experience does not bear out Min's assertion that borrowers would be unable to refinance. Borrowers could hedge the interest-rate risk by locking in a forward rate in advance of renewal. German lenders offer forward rates up to five years—certainly U.S. lenders could do the same, given the deep derivative market. Alternatively, borrowers can adjust the degree of risk by varying the length of the fixed-rate period.

A complete and robust housing-finance system should offer borrowers a menu of mortgage options, ranging from short-term ARMs for borrowers who can handle payment change to long-term FRMs for borrowers who value payment stability. To assert that the FRM is the preferred alternative for most borrowers is naïve. Many borrowers have shorter-term time horizons and can handle some interest-rate risk. The reason borrowers select a longer-term fixed rate is the fact that government guarantees subsidize the rate. International experience does not support Min's assertion that the switch to shorter-duration instruments would lead to massive defaults if and when interest rates increase.

The prohibition of prepayment penalties on fixed-rate mortgages is also misguided. Borrowers should be given a choice—long-term versus short-term fixed rates, with and without prepayment penalties. The market will price the differences, giving price breaks to those borrowers willing and able to handle interest-rate risk. Following Canadian and European tradition, the imposition of a prepayment penalty should be limited. It should not apply to borrowers moving house, and it should be limited in term.[31]

The most important result of a shift away from the FRM would be a reduction in taxpayer liability for mortgage risk. There is nothing so special about housing finance that government should absorb the credit risk of the vast majority of the mortgage market or underwrite the interest-rate risk of that market. Two episodes of massive taxpayer losses should convince us of that fact.

NOTES

1. David Min, "Future of Housing Finance Reform: Why the 30-Year Fixed-Rate Mortgage Is an Essential Part of Our Housing Finance System" (memo, Center for American Progress, Washington, DC, November 19, 2010), http://www.americanprogress.org/issues/2010/11/housing_reform.html.

2. Susan E. Woodward, "The Future of the Capital Markets: Connecting Primary Consumer and Mortgage Credit Markets to Global Capital" (paper, Moving Forward: The Future of Consumer Credit and Mortgage Finance national symposium, Joint Center for Housing Studies, Harvard University, February 18–19, 2010), 7, http://www.jchs.harvard.edu/publications/MF10-4.pdf.

3. Adam J. Levitin and Susan M. Wachter, "Explaining the Housing Bubble," Research Paper No. 10-15, (Philadelphia: University of Pennsylvania Institute for Law & Economics, August 31, 2010) and Public Law Research Paper No. 10-60 (Washington, DC: Georgetown University Law Center, August 31, 2010), http://ssrn.com/abstract=1669401.

4. Savings and loans institutions (S&Ls) offered amortizing mortgages

through sinking-fund and level-payment arrangements. In 1930, such instruments accounted for approximately half of loans outstanding. Their average term was 11 years. See Morton Bodfish and A. Theobald, *Savings and Loan Principles* (Whitefish, MT: Kessinger Publishing, 1940).

5. Thomas N. Herzog, "History of Mortgage Finance with an Emphasis on Mortgage Insurance" (monograph, Society of Actuaries, Schaumburg, IL, 2009), http://www.soa.org/library/monographs/finance/housing-wealth/2009/september/mono-2009-mfi09-herzog-history.pdf. A 1935 amendment to the National Housing Act authorized a prepayment penalty equal to the lesser of 1 percent of the original mortgage amount or the amount of premium payments the borrower would have been required to pay if the FHA-insured mortgage had remained in force through its maturity date.

6. See Bodfish and Theobald, *Savings and Loan Principles*, for S&L complaints about FHA pricing.

7. S&Ls originated nongovernment insured loans but were subject to regulation that required fixed-rate lending—ostensibly for consumer protection reasons. Their lending was to borrowers who could not qualify for FHA loans (either due to underwriting or loan-size restrictions).

8. The sellers incurred an economic loss as investors purchased the loans at market prices. For regulatory accounting purposes, the seller could recognize the loss over the remaining term of the loan. Deferred loss accounting proved to be a poisoned chalice for many loans S&Ls. Not only did the policies lead them to sell their FRMs at the wrong time—when rates were high but falling—but also, the 1989 Financial Institutions Reform, Recovery, and Enforcement Act legislation eliminated deferred-loss accounting for regulatory capital purposes, rendering many institutions insolvent.

9. James Vickery analyzes the FRM/ARM market share as a function of the instruments' relative price, controlling for the term structure of interest rates and other time-series factors. He finds that a 20-basis point increase in the retail FRM interest rate is estimated to cause a 17 percentage point decline in the FRM market share. James Vickery, "Interest Rates and Consumer Choice in the Residential Mortgage Market" (working paper, Federal Reserve Bank of New York, September 2007), http://www.philadelphiafed.org/research-and-data/events/2007/consumer-credit-and-payments/papers/Vickery_07_Interest_Rates_and_Consumer_Mtg_Choice.pdf.

10. Interestingly, many ARMs have prepayment penalties, and Fannie and Freddie will enforce them.

11. John Krainer, "Mortgage Choice and the Pricing of Fixed-Rate and Adjustable-Rate Mortgages," *Federal Reserve Bank of San Francisco Newsletter*, February 2010, http://www.frbsf.org/publications/economics/letter/2010/el2010-03.html.

12. A plain-vanilla mortgage amortizes in 30 years or fewer, is fully documented, and has a "reasonable rate and fees." The FRM is a qualified mortgage, as is a vanilla ARM. However, the requirement that borrowers be qualified at the highest possible rate during the first five years of the term suggests that most qualified mortgages will be FRMs. Most ARMs, interest-only mortgages, and high-cost loans will be nonqualified. Qualified residential mortgages will be exempt from the requirement that loan sellers retain at least 5 percent of the risk. Risk retention will raise the cost of nonqualified mortgages, reducing their market share. See Michael Lea, *International Comparison of Mortgage Product Offerings*, Research Institute for Housing America, September 2010, http://www.housingamerica.org/RIHA/RIHA/Publications/74023_10122_Research_RIHA_Lea_Report.pdf.

13. ARMs have had a much worse default experience during the recession. In part, this reflects the predominance of ARMs in the subprime market. It also reflects a selection bias whereby riskier and more speculative borrowers went into ARMs. For an analysis of the latter, see Gadi Barlevy and Jonas D.M. Fisher, "Mortgage Choices and Housing Speculation" (working paper, Federal Reserve Bank of Chicago, November 2010), http://www.chicagofed.org/digital_assets/publications/working_papers/2010/wp2010_12.pdf.

14. Richard H. Thaler, "Mortgages Made Simpler," Economic View, *New York Times*, July 4, 2009, http://www.nytimes.com/2009/07/05/business/economy/05view.html.

15. Prepayment is not costless, however. There are significant transaction costs associated with refinancing. John Kiff compares Canadian and U.S. mortgage-origination costs and finds that the U.S. costs are three to five times higher for purchase loans and comparable for refinance loans (Canadian prepayment penalties are similar to the transactions costs of a U.S. transaction). Also, frequent refinancing often results in equity stripping, increasing the probability of future default. John Kiff, *Canadian Residential Mortgage Markets: Boring but Effective*, WP/09/130 (Washington, DC: International Monetary Fund, June 2009), http://www.imf.org/external/pubs/ft/wp/2009/wp09130.pdf.

16. The uncertainty about prepayment leads to considerable speculation on the future direction of mortgage rates that has little social benefit. Hedging also increases systemic risk through counterparty exposure. The huge hedge positions of Fannie and Freddie were one reason the government placed them in conservatorship in 2008.

17. Over the past 50 years, the average life of a 30-year mortgage has never been higher than 12 years (during periods of high interest rates) and often no more than 5 years (during periods of lower interest rates). Marshall Dennis and Thomas Pinkowish, *Residential Mortgage Lending: Principles and Practices*, 5th ed. (Cincinnati, OH: South-Western Educational

Publishing, 2004).

18. Lea, *International Comparison of Mortgage Product Offerings*.

19. Alex J. Pollock, "The Dark Side of the 30-Year Fixed-Rate Mortgage," *The American*, March 8, 2011.

20. This scenario occurred during the 1970s in the United States.

21. Hedging uncertain prepayment is both costly and risky. It leads to considerable speculation on the future direction of mortgage rates that has little social benefit. Hedging also increases systemic risk through counterparty exposure. The huge hedge positions of Fannie and Freddie were one reason the government placed them in conservatorship in 2008.

22. Hans-Joachim Dübel, "European Mortgage Markets: (Conjectures on) Macro Implications of Structural Idiosyncrasy," (presentation, DG ECFIN Conference, Berlin, November 21, 2005), http://ec.europa.eu /economy_finance/events/2005/bxlworkshop2111/contributions/duebel _en.pdf.

23. Mortgage shopping in the United States is also complicated by the use of points to adjust pricing. Borrowers are confronted with an array of rate and point combinations that differ across lenders. Points were introduced in the 1970s when market rates rose above FHA rate ceilings—another effect of government regulation.

24. Refinancing transactions costs could be eliminated with use of a "ratchet mortgage" in which the rate is automatically lowered without transaction costs. Bert Ely, "Why Mortgage Originators Should Offer Ratchet Mortgages" (presentation, Federal Housing Finance Agency, August 2010).

25. Although the popular press tended to focus on excessively risky nonresidential mortgage investments as the cause of the S&Ls' failure, the fact was that they were bankrupted by the asset-liability mismatch and tried to grow out of their earnings and capital problems through investment in high-risk assets.

26. The GSEs hold whole loans in their portfolios. They also repurchase securities they guarantee—in effect investing in the cash-flow risk associated with funding callable mortgages with a blend of callable and noncallable debts of different maturities.

27. Federal Housing Finance Agency (FHFA) projections of GSE losses found that most of the losses are due to their purchased loans rather than securities; see FHFA, "Projections Showing Range of Potential Draws for Fannie Mae and Freddie Mac," attachment to press release "FHFA Releases Projections Showing Range of Potential Draws for Fannie Mae and Freddie Mac," October 21, 2010.

28. Ibid., 11.

29. The Danes add a unique twist to the instrument in that the loan is backed

by an individual mortgage bond. If rates rise, the borrower can buy the bond at a discount and cancel the loan with the lender. This feature facilitates automatic deleveraging and reduces the likelihood of negative equity; see Michael Lea, *International Comparison of Mortgage Product Offerings*.

30. Canada supports its mortgage market through default insurance and cash-flow guarantees comparable to FHA insurance and Ginnie Mae guarantees in the United States. The market share of government-backed mortgages is considerably less, however, with approximately 50 percent of mortgages backed by government insurance and 25 percent of mortgages backed by guarantees. European countries—with the exception of the Netherlands—do not support their mortgage markets through insurance or guarantees.

31. For example, the maximum term over which the penalty applies is five years in Canada and the Netherlands and 10 years in Germany.

ABOUT THE CONTRIBUTORS

DWIGHT M. JAFFEE

DWIGHT M. JAFFEE is the Willis Booth Professor of Banking, Finance, and Real Estate at the Haas School of Business, University of California at Berkeley, where he has taught since 1991. He previously taught for many years in the economics department of Princeton University. Dr. Jaffee is a member of the Haas School's Finance and Real Estate group and is co-chair of the Fisher Center for Real Estate and Urban Economics, a UC Berkeley campus research center.

Dr. Jaffee's primary areas of research are real estate finance (especially mortgage backed securitization and the government-sponsored enterprises) and insurance (including financial guarantee, earthquakes, terrorism, and auto). Overall, he has authored six books and over 100 articles. Recent research papers in the real estate field relate to the subprime mortgage crisis, U.S. mortgage market policy, and the role of the government-sponsored enterprises. Recent research papers in the insurance field consider why private firms do not offer catastrophe insurance, the government's role in catastrophe insurance, and the structure of monoline insurers.

Dr. Jaffee has served in advisory roles for the World

Bank, the Federal Reserve System, the Office of Federal Housing Enterprise Oversight, and the U.S. Department of Housing and Urban Development. He is currently a public interest director on the Genworth Financial Contra Mutual Fund and a member of the Academic Advisory Board for Fitch Ratings.

Dr. Jaffee earned his BA in economics from Northwestern University and his PhD from the Massachusetts Institute of Technology.

ARNOLD KLING

ARNOLD KLING IS a member of the Financial Markets Working Group at the Mercatus Center at George Mason University. As a member of the working group, Dr. Kling draws on his experience at Freddie Mac and the Federal Reserve to increase understanding of monetary policy, the regulation "anomaly," and the inside workings of America's federal financial institutions.

Dr. Kling served as a senior economist at Freddie Mac from 1986–1994. He was an economist on the staff of the Board of Governors of the Federal Reserve System from 1980–1986. Previously, he started one of the first commercial websites, Homefair. He has taught economics and statistics at Berman Hebrew Academy in Rockville, MD, and economic citizenship at George Mason University in Fairfax, VA.

Dr. Kling has authored three books, *Learning Economics*, a collection of essays on economic issues, *Under the Radar*, and *Crisis of Abundance: Rethinking How We Pay for Health Care*. He coauthors EconLog with Brian Caplan and David Henderson and has testified before Congress on the collapse of Fannie Mae and Freddie Mac.

Dr. Kling received his PhD in economics from the Massachusetts Institute of Technology.

MICHAEL LEA

DR. MICHAEL LEA is the director of The Corky McMillin Center for Real Estate at San Diego State University. In that capacity, he is responsible for improving real estate education, industry outreach, and research. He is also a visiting professor of finance. Previous to his current position, Dr. Lea taught at Cornell University; San Diego State University; the University of California, San Diego; and the Wharton International Housing Finance Program at the University of Pennsylvania.

Dr. Lea also has over 25 years of financial services industry experience, including more than 18 years of international advisory work in 28 countries spanning six continents. He has also held senior executive positions at several major financial institutions in the United States.

An internationally known authority on housing and mortgage finance, Dr. Lea has written over 75 articles, publications, and book chapters, including an influential World Bank publication on emerging market housing finance. His current research interests are comparative housing finance systems, the future of the government-sponsored enterprises, and solutions to the mortgage market crisis.

Dr. Lea received his PhD in economics from the University of North Carolina, Chapel Hill.

ANTHONY B. SANDERS

ANTHONY B. SANDERS is a senior scholar at the Mercatus Center at George Mason University and the Distinguished Professor of Real Estate Finance in the School of Management at George Mason University. He previously taught at University of Chicago (Graduate School of Business), University of Texas at Austin (McCombs School of Business), and The Ohio State University (Fisher College of Business). In addition, he served as director and head of asset-backed and mortgage-backed securities research at Deutsche Bank in New York City.

Dr. Sanders's research and teaching focuses on financial institutions and capital markets with particular emphasis on real estate finance and investment. He has published articles in *Journal of Finance*, *Journal of Financial and Quantitative Analysis*, *Journal of Business*, *Journal of Financial Services Research*, and *Journal of Housing Economics* among others. He serves as associate editor for several leading journals, has presented worldwide on the subject of the housing bubble and commercial real estate in the U.S. and the mortgage market, and has testified before the U.S. Senate and U.S. House of Representatives on the U.S. real estate asset and debt markets.

Dr. Sanders earned his PhD and MA from the University of Georgia.

PETER J. WALLISON

PETER J. WALLISON holds the Arthur F. Burns Chair in Financial Policy Studies and is co-director of AEI's program on financial policy studies. Prior to joining AEI, he practiced banking, corporate, and financial law at Gibson, Dunn & Crutcher in Washington, DC, and New York. Mr. Wallison also held a number of government positions. From June 1981 to January 1985, he was general counsel of the U.S. Treasury Department, where he played a significant role in the development of the Reagan administration's proposals for deregulation in the financial services industry. During 1986 and 1987, Mr. Wallison was White House counsel to President Ronald Reagan.

Mr. Wallison is the author of several books, including *Ronald Reagan: The Power of Conviction and the Success of His Presidency* and *Back from the Brink*, a proposal for a private deposit insurance system. He is coauthor of several others, most notably *Nationalizing Mortgage Risk: The Growth of Fannie Mae and Freddie Mac* and *The GAAP Gap: Corporate Disclosure in the Internet Age*. Mr. Wallison is a frequent contributor to the op-ed pages of the *Washington Post*, *Wall Street Journal*, and *Financial Times* and has also been a speaker at many conferences on financial services, accounting, and corporate governance. He is a member of the Shadow Financial Regulatory Committee, the Council on Foreign Relations, the SEC Advisory Committee on Improvements to Financial Reporting (2008), and the congressionally authorized Financial Crisis Inquiry Commission. He is also cochair of the Financial Reform Task Force.

Mr. Wallinson received his undergraduate degree from Harvard College and his law degree from Harvard Law School.

LAWRENCE J. WHITE

LAWRENCE J. WHITE is a member of the Financial Markets Working Group at the Mercatus Center at George Mason University. He is Arthur E. Imperatore Professor of Economics at New York University's Stern School of Business and deputy chair of the economics department at Stern. During 1986–1989, he was on leave to serve as board member, Federal Home Loan Bank Board and in that capacity was also a board member of Freddie Mac. During 1982–1983, he was on leave to serve as director of the Economic Policy Office, Antitrust Division, U.S. Department of Justice. He is currently the general editor of *The Review of Industrial Organization* and secretary-treasurer of the Western Economic Association International. Dr. White also served on the senior staff of the President's Council of Economic Advisers during 1978–1979 and was chairman of the Stern School's Department of Economics, 1990–1995.

He is the author of several books, including *The Automobile Industry Since 1945*; *Industrial Concentration and Economic Power in Pakistan*; *Reforming Regulation: Processes and Problems*; and *The S&L Debacle: Public Policy Lessons for Bank and Thrift Regulation*, as well as numerous articles in leading economics and law journals. He is also the editor or co-editor of eleven volumes and was the North American editor of *The Journal of Industrial Economics* from 1984–1987 and 1990–1995. He is a coauthor of the recently published *Guaranteed to Fail: Fannie Mae, Freddie Mac and the Debacle of Mortgage Finance*.

Dr. White earned his BA from Harvard University, MSc from the London School of Economics, and PhD from Harvard University.

INDEX

Page numbers in italics indicate tables and figures; the letter n following a page number indicates a note.

AAA-rated investments, 47, 82
Acharya, Viral, 49
adjustable-rate mortgages (ARMs)
    defaults, 192n13
    depository institutions, 137
    vs. FRMs, 42
    history, 175
    interest-rate risk, 126–127, 144n12
    international comparisons, 42, 56n20, *157t*, 185, *186t*
    market share, 42, 175, 191n9
    mortgage pricing, *178t*
    nonqualified mortgages, 192n12
    prepayment penalties, 191n10
    subprime market, 192n13
affordability gap, 9
affordable housing
    current GSE requirements, 84, 100
    as public policy objective, 63, 84, 162
    removal from GSE goals, 73–74, 133, 150n50, 162, 164

Alt-A loans
    delinquency rates, 103
    GSE holdings, 94, 97, 109, *110t*
    increasing homeownership rates, 106
    increasing housing bubble, 109
    outstanding loans, *110t*, 111
ARMs. *see* adjustable-rate mortgages
asset-liability mismatch, 71, 80, 183, 193n25

banks. *see* depository institutions
Barclays Capital, 96
Bernanke, Ben S., 48
bonds, covered. *see* covered bonds
borrowers, credit risk factors, 15n4, 125, 144nn9–11
Bush (G.W.) administration, affordable-housing goals, 94

Canada
    mortgage duration, 79–80

mortgage-market support, 155, 194n30
mortgage-origination costs, 192n15
prepayment penalty, 178, 194n31
rollover mortgages, 170n23, 185
capital gains tax exemptions, 39, 146n31
capital requirements, 70, 77, 81, 168n4, 170n24
Case Shiller Index, *153f*
cash-out refinancing, 65
catastrophic insurance, 141
CBO (Congressional Budget Office) reform proposals, 48–49
Cembalest, Michael, 9
Chirui, Maria Conceeta, 32–33
Clinton administration, affordable-housing goals, 94
CMBS (commercial mortgage-backed securities) market, 169n15
Coles, Adrian, 58n30
collateral
  and credit risk, 124, 144n5
  mortgages as, 80, 128, 137, 142, 143n1
  in tranching structures, 40, 130, 131, 139
commercial mortgage-backed securities (CMBS) market, 169n15
Committee on Financial Services, U.S. House of Representatives, 9–10, 15n10
community governance, involvement in, 133, 146n30
Community Reinvestment Act (CRA), 109, *110t*

conforming loan limit
  in high-cost areas, 97, 100, 147n40, 163
  reduction proposals, 19–20, 49, 52, 116, 117, 120, 140, 150n58, 163–164, 170n21
conforming loans
  default rates, 152
  mortgage rates, 167
Congressional Budget Office (CBO) mortgage reform proposals, 48–49
corporatism, 83
covered bonds
  Danish system, 159–160
  definition, 80
  German system, 159–160, 169n9, 169n12
  interest-rate risk, 169n12
  local government backing, 58n31
  and overcollateralization, 169n10
  potential investors, 147n38
  protection against credit losses, 40, 41
  as securitization alternative, 26
  as single-class obligation, 40
  in U.S. market, 53
CRA (Community Reinvestment Act), 109, *110t*
credit history, and credit risk, 15n4, 125
credit rating agencies, 131
credit risk
  addressing, 127–132
  basics, 124–126
  and credit history, 15n4, 125
  default costs, 144n6
  FHA, 109

FRMs, 184
GSEs, 94, 109
interest-rate risk, 131–132
securitization structure, 128–131
traditional lending structures, 128
crony capitalism, 83–84

debt-to-income ratio, 113
defaults. see mortgage defaults
deferred-loss accounting, 191n8
Denmark
bank failures, 169n14
covered bonds, 40, 160
FRMs, 42, 185
mortgage bonds, 193n29
mortgage- financing system, 113–114
deposit insurance system, 120n9. see also Federal Deposit Insurance Corporation (FDIC)
deposit interest-rate caps, 93
depository institutions
access to long-term funding, 82
ARMs and nonstandard mortgages, 137
capital requirements, 136, 147n37
crony capitalism, 83–84
funding costs, 80
GSE advantages over, 136–137
hedging strategies, 84, 131–132
historical accounting, 80–81
interest-rate risk, 80–81, 84–85, 86
Jimmy Stewart banker approach, 84–85
lending decisions, 83
local orientation, 145n19
maturity mismatching, 80
mortgage-market share, 22f, 23, 25, 136–137, 147n36
portfolio lending, 46, 53, 161
private mortgage-finance system, 136–137
regulation deficiencies, 48
risky loans, 9
traditional lending structure, 23–24, 128
Desktop Originator and Underwriter (computer software), 55n10
devil-you-know approach to reform, 68–78
advantages, 61, 75
risks, 75–77
disappearing yields problem, 13
Dodd-Frank financial reform (2010), 84, 168n7, 175
down payments
after elimination of GSEs, 166
Jimmy Stewart banker approach, 85
minimal, 2, 65–66
and owner-occupancy rates, 32–33
prime mortgages, 112
private mortgage insurance, 88n7
size, 8, 74, 112
standard, 88n7

Ellen, Ingrid Gould, 49
employment history, and credit risk, 125
equity. see home equity
Europe. see Western Europe
European Central Bank, 35–36
European Mortgage Federation, 28n1, 31, 39

European Union
  prohibition against subsidies, 39, 56n16
  tax benefits, 58n29
"excess spread," 131
exotic mortgage instruments, 65, 74, 150n57
extension risk, 181

Fannie Mae. *see also* government-sponsored enterprises
  affordable-housing loans, 94, 100, 164
  asset-liability mismatch, 183
  average debt spread, *11f*
  bailout and conservatorship, 17, 151, 192n16, 193n21
  bankruptcy, 71, 89n10
  capital requirement, 168n4
  charter, 94, 97, 120n4
  conforming loan limit, 97, 163–164
  credit risk, 94
  delinquency rates, 103, 111
  eliminated in reform proposals, 115–119, 163–167
  elimination of nonmortgage investments, 165
  franchise value, 161, 170n19
  future, 151–170
  guarantee on securities, 96
  hedge positions, 192n16, 193n21
  high LTV ratio loans, 8
  history, 92, 93–94, 174
  implicit government guarantee, 130
  interest-rate risk, 71
  MBS, 24, 145n21
  mortgage-market share, 151
  multifamily housing mortgages, 143n2
  outstanding subprime and Alt-A loans, *110t*
  political power, 64, 76–77, 88n3
  prepayment penalties, 168n6, 175, 191n10
  prime mortgages, 164
  privatization, 3–4, 93, 161–162
  public-private hybrid, 24
  retained portfolios, 164–165
  risk-taking, 4
  single-family residential mortgages, 143n2
  underwriting standards, 55n10, 97
FDIC. *see* Federal Deposit Insurance Corporation
Federal Credit Reform Act, 114
Federal Deposit Insurance Corporation (FDIC), 51, 86, 98, 120n9, 169n10
Federal Emergency Management Agency (FEMA), 121n10
Federal Home Loan Bank System (FHLBS), 55n5, 55n12, 147n38
Federal Housing Administration (FHA)
  claim rate, 96
  credit risk, 94, 109
  FRMs, 173
  Ginnie Mae guarantees, 129–130
  high-risk loans, 109
  history, 7, 173
  loan ceiling, 147n40
  low-income borrowers, 20, 37, 52, 95, 114, 148n45
  mortgage insurance, 21, 51–52, 91–92, 95–97, 174

mortgage-market share, 151
mortgage-market support, 17,
    18, 54n4
mortgage quality standards,
    114–115
in mortgage reform proposals,
    18, 49, 52, 89n14,
    114–115, 147n35
outstanding subprime and Alt-A
    loans, *110t*
taxpayer costs, 96
underwriting standards, 95
Federal Housing Finance Agency
    (FHFA)
GSE loss projections, 95, 184,
    193n27
Federal Reserve
interest rates, 175
Regulation Q, 93
responsibilities, 150n53
retained portfolios, 165
Truth in Lending regulations, 45
Federal Savings and Loan Insurance
    Corporation, 120n9
FEMA (Federal Emergency
    Management Agency),
    121n10
FHA. *see* Federal Housing
    Administration
FHLBS. *see* Federal Home Loan Bank
    System
FICO score, 15n4
financial concentration, 83
financial crises
mortgages as cause, 7
prevention, 150n51
Financial Institutions Reform,
    Recovery, and
    Enforcement Act (1989),
    191n8
first-time home buyers, 18, 147n35

five-year rollover mortgages, 79–80
fixed-rate mortgages (FRM). *see
    also* 30-year fixed-rate
    mortgages
vs. ARMs, 42
benefits to borrowers, 171–172,
    176
costs, 177–184, 188
credit risk, 184
funding instruments, 81–82
gold standard myth, 184–188
government guarantees,
    183–184
history, 173–176
interest-rate risk, 126, 127, 131,
    144n13, 181
international comparisons, *157t*,
    185, *186t*
investors, 75–76
market dominance, 168n7,
    171–172
market share, 171, 191n9
mortgage interest rates, 146n29,
    181
mortgage pricing, *178t*
negative equity, 179, 181
prepayment, 43, 156, 168n6,
    175, 176, 185
qualified mortgages, 192n12
refinancing, 176, 183
short-term, *157t*, *186t*
subsidies, 172
flood insurance, 51, 98, 121n10,
    150n52
foreclosures. *see also* mortgage
    defaults
challenges to, 75
costs, 45
history, 111
Jimmy Stewart banker approach,
    78–79

prime mortgages, 35
subprime mortgages, 35
Western Europe vs. U.S., *32t*,
34–35, *187t*
France
   FRMs, 185
Freddie Mac. *see also* government-sponsored enterprises (GSEs)
   affordable-housing loans, 94, 100, 164
   average debt spread, *11f*
   bailout and conservatorship, 17, 151, 192n16, 193n21
   capital requirement, 168n4
   charter, 94, 97
   conforming loan limit, 97, 163–164
   credit risk, 94
   delinquency rates, 103, 111
   eliminated in reform proposals, 115–119, 163–167
   franchise value, 161, 170n19
   future, 151–170
   hedge positions, 192n16, 193n21
   history, 24, 93–94, 174
   implicit government guarantee, 96, 130
   interest-rate risk, 71
   MBS, 24, 145n21
   mortgage-market share, 151
   multifamily housing mortgages, 143n2
   nonmortgage investments, 165
   one-year ARMs, *29t*, 33, 56n20
   outstanding subprime and Alt-A loans, *110t*
   political power, 64, 76–77, 88n3
   prepayment penalties, 168n6, 175, 191n10
   prime mortgages, 164
   privatization, 3–4, 161–162
   retained portfolios, 164–165
   risk-taking, 4
   single-family residential mortgages, 143n2
   30-year fixed rate mortgages, *182f*
   underwriting standards, 55n10, 97
FRMs. *see* fixed-rate mortgages; 30-year fixed-rate mortgages
Fugate, Craig, 121n10

GAO. *see* Government Accountability Office
Germany
   FRMs, 185
   hyperinflation, 169n13
   interest rates, 189
   mortgage-financing system, 114
   Pfandbrief (covered bonds), 159–160, 169n9, 169n12
   prepayment penalty, 194n31
Ginnie Mae (GNMA)
   expansion, 137–138
   guarantees, 24, 94, 129–130, 147n40
   history, 24, 174
   loan limits, 148n45
   MBS, 24, 145n20
   mortgage-market support, 18, 54n4
   reform proposals, 147n35
Ginsberg, Jodie, 57n24
GNMA. *see* Ginnie Mae
"gold standard" conforming loans, 152

Government Accountability Office (GAO)
  reform proposals, 48–49
Government National Mortgage Association. *see* Ginnie Mae
government-sponsored enterprises (GSEs). *see also* Fannie Mae; Freddie Mac
  advantages over depository institutions, 1, 136–137
  Alt-A loans, 109, *110t*
  arguments against, 50–52, 70–71, 106–107
  arguments for, 3, 68, 101–103, 106–107
  bailout and conservatorship, 9–10, 15n10, 17, 27, 30, 77, 145n23
  borrowers' income, 66
  callable debt, 81
  capital requirements, 70, 73, 136, 147n37, 167
  and Case Shiller Index, *153f*
  charters, 21, 63
  conforming loan limit, 68, 100, 140, 147n40
  conforming loan limit reduction, 19–20, 52, 116, 117
  contract design, 21, 44–45
  credit losses, 72
  credit risk, 109
  crony capitalism, 83–84
  deficiencies, 98–101
  definition, 55n12
  delinquency rates, 111
  elimination under reform proposals, 18–31, 79, 86–87, 115–119
  expansion, 17, 100, 137–138, 147n40
  FRM inventory, 184
  guarantee fees, 20, 140
  guarantees as moral hazard, 1, 97, 99
  high-risk loans, 9, 62, 109
  history, 93–95
  implicit guarantees, 1, 24, 27
  interest-rate risk, 42, 70–72
  international equivalents, 38–39, 155
  limitations, 150n57
  loss projections, 184, 193n27
  loss reserving, 70
  MBS, 17, 27, 42
  middle-market mortgages, 38–39
  mission, 62–68, 74
  mortgage-market revival, 18
  mortgage-market share, 9, *22f*, 23, 25, 46, 154
  mortgage origination, 21
  mortgage portfolio, 56n13, 143n1, 148n44, 193n26
  mortgage-processing standards, 68–69
  mortgage rates, 68, 88n8
  multifamily housing mortgages, 55n6, 143n2
  organizational capital, 61, 78
  prepayment risk exposure, 81
  prime loans, 111
  regulatory oversight, 61, 63–64, 72, 73, 77
  replacement by private markets, 123
  risk-based pricing, 70
  risk-management tools, 68, 70
  risk-taking, 1–2, 66

role in financial crisis, 7–10
role in reform proposals, 67–68, 74, 87, 141–142, 149n49, 152–155
single-family residential mortgages, 143n2
as stabilizing force, 89n11
subprime loans, 109, *110t*
taxpayer costs, 54, 94–95, 106
underwriting standards, 8, 21, 55n10, 68–69, 102–103
Western Europe vs. U.S., *35t*
yield on debt, 13
Great Depression, 92–93
Great Recession, 134
GSE. see government-sponsored enterprises
GSE Act. see Housing and Community Development Act

Hancock, Diana, 49
Hardt, Judith, 58n30
hedge funds, as mortgage investors, 138
high-risk bond mutual funds, as mortgage investors, 138
Home Buyers' Tax Credit, 3
home equity
 accumulation, 8, 64, 88n4
 dissipation, 8, 67, 192n15
 negative equity, 144n8, 179, *180f*, 181
 prime-quality mortgages, 112–113
Home Mortgage Interest Deduction, 2, 39, 54n4, 146n31
homeownership. see also owner-occupancy rates
 after elimination of GSEs, 166
 historic rates, 92, 106–107, 157, *158f*
 public policy objectives, 5, 62–68, 74, 157–159
 social costs, 10–13
 social value, 12, 64–65, 133
 Western Europe vs. U.S., 107
house prices
 GSE phase-out proposal, 87, 166
 history, 7, *108f*
 home-price index (1993-2011), *6f*
 house-price inflation, *105t*
 housing bubbles, 107, 109
 housing-finance system goals, 133
 Jimmy Stewart banker approach, 85
 median, 117, 147n40
 and negative equity, *180f*
 volatility, *28t*, 33
 Western Europe vs. U.S., *28t*
Housing and Community Development Act (1992), 94
Housing and Economic Recovery Act (2008), 97, 100
housing bubbles, 107, 109, 111, 112, 134–135
housing collapse, 65, 134–135
housing construction industry, *28t*, 33, 102, *104t*, 134
housing-finance system
 appropriate goals, 132–133
 basics, 124–132
 developed and developing countries, 57n26
 government involvement, 7, 91–98
 inappropriate goals, 133
 international examples, 113–114

Wall Street role, 84
housing-finance system reform
    CBO proposal, 48–49
    decentralization, 62
    devil-you-know approach, 68–78
    Fannie Mae role, 115–119, 163–167
    FHA role, 18, 49, 52, 89n14, 114–115, 147n35
    Freddie Mac role, 115–119, 163–167
    GAO proposal, 48–49
    GNMA role, 147n35
    goals, 66–67, 155–162
    GSEs' elimination, 18–31, 79, 86–87, 115–119
    GSEs' role, 67–68, 74, 87, 141–142, 149n49, 152–155
    HUD/Treasury proposal, 18, 19, 49, 52, 55n5, 147n34, 149n49
    implementation, 140–142
    Jimmy Stewart banker approach, 62, 78–85
    LMI loans, 52, 65, 67, 147n35
    MBS, 49–50
    mortgage interest rates, 54
    mortgage investors, 46–47
    mortgage originators, 44
    national property-recording database, 74–75
    Obama administration plan, 99, 152, 154
    private-market incentives, 17–59
    privatization, 19–20, 135–139
    regulatory mechanisms, 47–48, 73, 77–78
    risk-based pricing, 53–54
    side-by-side government guarantee, 141–142
    Treasury Department role, 73
    Truth in Lending Act, 48
    underwriting standards, 44–46, 49, 50
    VA role, 89n14, 147n35
HUD. see U.S. Department of Housing and Urban Development
Hurricane Katrina, 51

income redistribution, 67, 133
income tax benefits. see Home Buyers' Tax Credit; Home Mortgage Interest Deduction; tax benefits
individual mortgage bonds, 194n29
inflation (1970s), 80
interest rates
    on deposits, 80
    prepayable mortgages, 178
interest-rate derivatives, 132
interest-rate risk
    addressing, 131–132
    ARMs, 144n12
    basics, 126–127
    covered bonds, 169n12
    depository institutions, 80–81
    distribution, 58n32, 84
    GSEs, 42, 70–72
    hedging, 131–132
    regulation, 84
interest-rate volatility, 181, 183
International Monetary Fund, 85
Ireland
    housing downturn, 186
    mortgage defaults, 35

Jaffee, Dwight M., 1, 106, 144n13, 146n29

Japan
    FRMs, 185
    government-supported mortgages, 155
Jappelli, Tullio, 32–33
Jimmy Stewart banker approach to reform, 78–85
    decentralizing mortgage-finance system, 62
    implementation considerations, 84–85
    reducing government involvement, 62
jumbo loan market, 68, 101–102

Kiff, John, 192n15

Lea, Michael, 56n15
lending standards
    weakening of, 8
    to address affordability gap, 9
Levitin, Adam, 171
life insurance companies, as mortgage investors, 55n11, 138, 147n38
LMI. *see* low-and-moderate income (LMI) loans
LoanProspector (computer software), 55n10
loan-to-value (LTV) ratio, 8–9, 92, 124–125
long-term fixed rate mortgages. *see also* fixed-rate mortgages; 30-year fixed-rate mortgages
    international comparisons, *157t, 186t*
low-and-moderate income (LMI) loans
    FHA and HUD programs, 18, 20, 37–38, 114–115
    GSEs, 20, 100
    as high-risk loans, 109
    need for government backing, 103
    in reform proposals, 52, 65, 67, 114–115, 147n35
    Title XIII, 94
low-quality mortgages, market for, 110
LTV. *see* loan-to-value (LTV) ratio

Maloni, Bill, 88n3
market investors
    definition, 25
    mortgage-market share, *22f*, 23, 25
MBS. *see* mortgage-backed securities
medium-term fixed rate mortgages
    international comparisons, *157t, 186t*
Mercer Oliver Wyman (consulting firm), 57n26
middle-market mortgages, 37, 38–39
Mills, Edwin S., 12
Min, David, 171, 177, 184, 186, 187
Monetary Control Act (1980), 93
moral-hazard problems, 70, 97, 99, 126
mortgage-backed securities (MBS). *see also* private-label mortgage-backed securities
    "agency," 24
    capital requirement, 168n4
    credit risk, 40–41, 129
    demand for, 7, 83
    government guarantees, 42, 49, 100, 145nn20–21

history, 24
by holder class, *22f*
interest-rate risk, 42
multi-class structured format, 40–41, 58n32
in reform proposals, 49–50
side-by-side government guarantee, 142, 150n56
third-party guarantees, 131
mortgage credit
distribution, 66
as income redistribution tool, 67
restructuring, 82
mortgage defaults. *see also* foreclosures
ARMs, 192n13
and conforming loan limit, 152
costs, 45–46
and down payment size, 65
financial-sector impact, 135
political intervention, 69
recourse, 43
reputational costs, 144n7
and second mortgages, 144n9
and underwriting standards, 69–70, 160
Western Europe vs. U.S., *32t*, 34–35, 43, *187t*
mortgage delinquency, 103, 111–112
mortgage denials, 69–70
mortgage duration
average, 19
in Canada, 79–80
and credit risk, 125
mortgage insurance programs, 51–52
mortgage interest rates
after elimination of GSEs, 27, 54, 56n14, 139, 166, 167
capital requirements, 170n24
conforming loans, 167
by country, *28t–29t, 29t*
fluctuation, 27
FRMs, 146n29
GSEs, 27, 68, 88n8, 116–117, 168n2
jumbo loan market, 68
net interest rate, 56n21
nongovernmental rate, 116–117
and prepayment, 43, 146n29
risk-based pricing, 30, 45, 46
Western Europe vs. U.S., *28t–29t*, 30–31, 33–34, 57n22, *105t*, 106
mortgage interest tax deduction. *see* Home Mortgage Interest Deduction
mortgage market. *see also* housing-finance system; private-mortgage market
alternative systems, 57n26
functional structure, 21–26, 57n23
fundamental features, 44
government support, 37–40
mortgage investment function, 23–26
national market, 96
performance without GSEs, 27, 30–31
reform proposals, 46–47
third-party sales, 70
Western Europe, 57n26
Western Europe vs. U.S., *28t–29t, 104t–105t*
mortgage origination
costs, 192n15
GSE standards, 70
impact of volatile interest rates on, 183

private-market incentives, 18
reform proposals, 21, 44
securitization model, 128, 129, 145n17
traditional lending structure, 128
mortgage-processing standards, 68–69
mortgage products
after elimination of GSEs, 166
mortgage pricing, *178t*
need for innovation, 155–156
points, 193n23
Western Europe vs. U.S., 41, *157t*, *186t*
mortgage refinancing. *see* refinancing
mortgage securitization. *see* securitization
mortgage underwriting. *see* underwriting standards
mortgage-finance system. *see* housing-finance system
multifamily housing mortgages, 55n6, 143n2

National Flood Insurance Program (NFIP), 51, 98, 121n10
National Housing Act (1934), 173, 191n5
national property-recording database, 74–75
negative equity, 144n8, 179, *180f*, 181
net interest rate, 56n21
Netherlands
government-supported mortgages, 155, 194n30
prepayment penalty, 194n31
Neuteboom, Peter, 56n21
Nevins, Lou, 88n3

NFIP. *see* National Flood Insurance Program
nonhousing investments
rate of return, 12
social rate of return, 12–13
nontraditional mortgages. *see* risky loans

Obama administration
reform plan, 99, 152, 154
report on future of mortgage finance, 143n1
OECD (Organisation for Economic Co-operation and Development), 33
Office of Federal Housing Enterprise Oversight (OFHEO), 72
Organisation for Economic Co-operation and Development (OECD), 33
outstanding mortgage-to-GDP ratio, *28t–29t*, 34, *105t*
outstanding subprime and Alt-A loans, *110t*, 111
overcollateralization, 131, 169n10
owner-occupancy rates. *see also* homeownership
during mortgage-lending frenzy, 64
relationship to down-payment rates, 32–33
Western Europe vs. U.S., *28t*, 31–32, *104t*

Passmore, Wayne, 49
"pass-through" securities, 145n16
Paulson, Henry, 77
Pension Benefit Guaranty Corporation (PBGC), 98
pension funds, as mortgage investors, 138, 147n38

Pfandbrief (covered bonds), 159–160, 169n9
Pinto, Edward, 8–9, 109
PLMBS. *see* private-label mortgage-backed securities
points (price-adjustment mechanism), 193n23
political intervention
   GSEs, 64, 68, 76–77, 83–84, 88n3
   mortgage defaults, 69
   mortgage denials, 69
Pollock, Alex J., 179
portfolio lending, 161
prepayment feature
   costs, 172, 178–179, 187–188, 192n15
   FRMs, 175, 176
   interest-rate risk, 127, 132, 144n13
   and mortgage interest rates, 146n29, 178
   risk management, 177, 192n16, 193n21
prepayment penalties
   ARMs, 191n10
   authorization, 191n5
   commercial mortgages, 43
   enforcement, 191n10
   FRMs, 156, 185
   international comparisons, 43, 194n31
   prohibitions, 42–43, 168n6, 190
prime-quality mortgages
   definition, 8
   delinquency rates, 103, 111–112
   features, 112–113
   GSEs, 164
   home equity, 112–113
   regulation, 112–113

private-label mortgage-backed securities (PLMBS)
   crash, 137–138
   mortgage collateral, 40
   revival, 160–161
   securitization, 147n39
Private Label Securities (PLS), 24–25, 26, 137–139
private mortgage insurance (PMI), 47, 51, 88n7
private-mortgage market
   capital requirements, 167
   competition with GSEs, 13, 45
   expanded menu of choices, 45, 53
   interaction with public capital, 15n17, 18
   likely structure and performance, 44–48
   Obama reform plan, 99
   recovery, 159–162
   reforming mortgage market through incentives, 17–59
   replacing GSEs, 13, 20, 123
   Western Europe, 38–39
property-recording database, 74–75

qualified residential mortgages (QRMs), 168n7, 175, 176, 192n12

ratchet mortgages, 193n24
real-estate industry, 3, 134
recourse and limited mortgage defaults, 43
refinancing
   cash-out refinancing, 65
   equity stripping, 192n15
   and falling housing prices, 179
   FRMs, 176, *182f*

and interest-rate volatility, 181, 183
options, 156
origination fees, 183
risk to GSEs, 81
transaction costs, 193n24
volume, *182f*
reform proposals. *see* housing-finance system reform
Regulation Q, 93
regulatory oversight
deficiencies, 48
depository institutions, 48
Federal Reserve, 45, 93
GSEs, 61, 63–64, 72, 73, 77, 87
HUD, 77
interest-rate risk, 84
prime-quality mortgages, 112–113
reform proposals, 47–48, 73, 77–78, 84–85, 87
securitized mortgages, 112–113
subprime crisis, 48
Treasury Department, 73
Truth in Lending regulations, 45
Western Europe, 42–43
residential mortgage-backed securities (RMBS) market, 154
residential property values. *see* house prices
return on investment, 12
Richardson, Matthew, 49
risk-based pricing, 50–51, 53–54, 65, 70
risk-free investments, demand for, 46–47
risky loans, 9

RMBS. *see* residential mortgage-backed securities (RMBS) market
rollover mortgages, 166, 170n23, 185, 189

Sallie Mae, 55n5
Salomon (bank), 88n3
savings and loan (S&L) industry
amortizing mortgages, 190n4
ARMs, 175
asset-liability mismatch, 183, 193n25
credit risk, 146n27
crisis, 80–81, 183, 193n25
FRMs, 174, 191n7, 191n8
history, 92–93
interest-rate risk, 71, 131, 146n27
second mortgages, 65, 113, 144n9
secondary mortgage market, 174
securitization
adverse consequences, 83–84
credit risk, 128–131
history, 24
private-market incentives, 18
regulation, 112–113
success, 26
Wall Street's role, 84
short-term fixed rate mortgages, *157t, 186t*
side-by-side government guarantee, 141–142, 150n56
social rate of return, 12–13
Spain
covered bonds, 40
foreclosure rate, 35
Stewart, Jimmy. *see* Jimmy Stewart banker approach to reform
stock market collapse, 135

stress-test simulations, 61, 70, 72, 73, 77, 84–85
subprime mortgages
　ARM dominance, 192n13
　delinquency rates, 103
　losses, 26
　outstanding loans, 111
　subprime crisis, 26, 48, 137
Summers, Lawrence, 63–64
"swap" concept, 174
Sweden
　covered bonds, 40

"tail-risk" insurance, 141, 148n48
tax benefits. see also Home Buyers' Tax Credit; Home Mortgage Interest Deduction
　capital-gain rules, 39, 146n31
　state property tax deduction, 39
　Western Europe, 39, 58n29
Taylor, Lori, 12–13
technology stocks, collapse of, 134–135
30-year fixed-rate mortgages
　availability, 101–102
　average life, 192n17
　interest-rate premium, 82
　investors, 75–76
　market dominance, 156–157
　mortgage pricing, *178t*
　vs. mortgage refinance volume, *182f*
　necessity of, 171–194
　negative aspects, 156
thrift institutions, 55n11, 80. see also savings and loan (S&L) industry
Title XIII, 94
"too-big-to-fail" banks, 71

tranching, 130–131, 138–139, 145nn24–25
Treasury Department. see U.S. Department of the Treasury
Truth in Lending Act, 45, 48
Turner, Lorraine, 57n24
Tye, John Napier, 49

"under water" mortgages. see negative equity
underqualified buyers. see low-and-moderate income (LMI) loans
underwriting standards
　GSEs, 21, 23, 68–69, 102–103
　lack of incentive for, 83
　minimizing loan defaults, 160
　as mortgage-market function, 21
　reform proposals, 44–46, 49, 50
United Kingdom
　ARMs, 42
　foreclosure rate, 35
　tax deductions, 39
"upside down" mortgages. see negative equity
U.S. Department of Housing and Urban Development (HUD). see also Ginnie Mae
　affordable-housing goals, 63, 94
　Fannie Mae control, 88n3
　GNMA, 24
　GSE regulatory oversight, 77
　lower-income home buyer programs, 20, 37, 52, 66
　mission, 72–73
　mortgage-market reform white paper, 19, 49, 52, 55n5, 147n34, 149n49

mortgage-market support, 54n4
outstanding subprime and Alt-A loans, *110t*
in reform proposals, 18
U.S. Department of the Treasury
GSE bailout, 145n23
mortgage-market reform white paper, 19, 49, 52, 55n5, 147n34, 149n49
in reform proposals, 73
U.S. Department of Veterans Affairs (VA)
Ginnie Mae guarantees, 129–130
history, 174
mortgage-market activity, 17–18
mortgage origination, 21
reform proposals, 89n14, 147n35

VA. *see* U.S. Department of Veterans Affairs
Van Nieuwerburgh, Stijn, 49
variable-rate mortgages. *see* adjustable-rate mortgages
Vickery, James, 191n9

Wachter, Susan, 171

Wallison, Peter J., 1
Western European mortgage and housing markets, 31–43
commercial bank holdings, 25–26
covered bonds, *38t*, 40–41
government intervention, *35t*, 37–40, 51, 57n27, 194n30
market success (safe mortgages), 41–43
mortgage choice, 41
mortgage defaults, *32t*, 35–36, 43
net interest rate, 56n21
owner-occupancy rates, *28t*, 31–32
performance, 31–36, *104t–105t*
prepayment penalties, 42–43, 178
recourse, 43
securitization, *38t*, 40–41
unique features, 36–41
U.S. comparisons, *28t–29t*
variable rate mortgages, 56n20
White, Lawrence J., 49
Willis, Mark A., 49
Woodard, Susan, 171

Made in the USA
Charleston, SC
24 June 2014